Legends, Tales, & Parables
A Witch's Book of Terribles

T0417974

About the Author

Wycke Malliway is an illustrator and a witch who has spent so long burried in myths and fairytales that he now lives one! In addition to being one of the founders of Crossed Crow Books, Wycke is also an owner of the Malliway Bros witchcraft shop located in Chicago with his brother, Blake. He is the primary facilitator of the Witches' Conclave, a Chicago-based group of magical practicioners who come together to learn and explore the various methods of making magic.

While he studies many forms of magic and lore, he specializes in folk magic traditions. The power connected to the land, unique local customs, and what spirits might reside in any given place have fueled not only this book, but his own brand of local witchery as well.

Legends, Tales, & Parables

A Witch's Book of Terribles

by Wycke Malliway

Chicago, IL

A Witch's Book of Terribles: Legends, Tales, & Parables
© 2025 by Wycke Malliway. All rights reserved. No part of this book may be reproduced in any manner whatsoever without written permission from Crossed Crow Books, except in the case of brief quotations embodied in critical articles and reviews.

Paperback ISBN: 978-1-959883-05-0
Hardcover ISBN: 978-1-964537-36-8
Library of Congress Control Number on file.

Cover design and illustrations by Wycke Malliway.
Typesetting by Wycke Malliway.
Edited by Kumari Pacheco.

Disclaimer: Crossed Crow Books, LLC does not participate in, endorse, or have any authority or responsibility concerning private business transactions between our authors and the public. Any internet references contained in this work were found to be valid during the time of publication, however, the publisher cannot guarantee that a specific reference will continue to be maintained. This book's material is not intended to diagnose, treat, cure, or prevent any disease, disorder, ailment, or any physical or psychological condition. The author, publisher, and its associates shall not be held liable for the reader's choices when approaching this book's material. The views and opinions expressed within this book are those of the author alone and do not necessarily reflect the views and opinions of the publisher.

Published by:
Crossed Crow Books, LLC
6934 N Glenwood Ave, Suite C
Chicago, IL 60626
www.crossedcrowbooks.com

Printed in the United States of America.
IBI

Contents:

Introduction: Enter the Crossroads... 7

Into the Witch's Woods... 10

Chapter One: Aunt Brynelda's Magical Trowel... 12

Are You a Witch?... 25

Chapter Two: Ipscingen of the Wishing Well... 26

The Ballad of Culfom Crau... 34

Chapter Three: Ditty Denna and the Dismal Duenna... 36

The Stregareum... 49

Chapter Four: The Lackadaisical Hare... 50

The Bending Wood... 69

Chapter Five: The Vanishing Hovel... 70

Always Waiting... 89

Chapter Six: Two Brothers and the Blood Wedding... 90

The Stars in Her Hair... 97

Chapter Seven: Neverfair... 98

Dandy's Dictum... 112

Chapter Eight: Behind White Lace... 114

Wayward Lines... 159

Chapter Nine: A Ledger of Wonders... 160

Afterword: Out of the Woods... 196

Appendix One: Terrible Storytelling... 197

Appendix Two: A Magical Menagerie... 204

Introduction
Enter the Crossroads

What could be learned from a witch? Royals have their fairy tales, gods have their myths, and creatures have their fables. But what about witches? What do they have to offer? Well, a witch is rarely the main character of those stories. They are the initiator, the spark that lights the flame, and the flame that lights the way. This book is for those sparks—for all who walk the crooked path. These lessons will not have much to garner for those who don't cobble in the magical arts themselves. If you do find yourself being especially drawn to these tales, however, then you may just have a bit of that spark kindling already.

As always, every witch's path is different, just as every witch is different. That's what makes our paths so crooked. What is fact to one might be a complete myth to another. But why should that make either more true than the next? Mystery and wonder are in every fiber of a witch's construction. Our power lies in whimsy and the unknown, the spin of a rhyme and the whispers of wood. So, does magic make the myth, or does myth make the magic? Either way, it's sure that the two will undoubtedly go hand in hand.

That is why I'm putting these lessons together into this batch of home-cooked folklore. Our methods might all be different, but experience is a language that any practice can understand. I've fumbled and grumbled through a lot in my own craft and have heard plenty of curious tales from other witches as well. I hope to pass on these magical beliefs, practical applications, and personal warnings through the experiences of the witches in this book. If you gain knowledge from my words, then that's excellent, but if you gain wisdom, even better! It will be up to your own imagination to decide what these stories truly mean.

With any luck, the adventures of these witches will lead you somewhere magical. Maybe you'll use them to avoid mishaps that you run into down the road. Or you might even be inspired to embark on an adventure of your own. Either way, you should savor your path for all that you find—the great, the small, the wonderful, or even the terrible. Because while witches might not have their own fairy tales, myths, or fables, we do indeed have our Terribles.

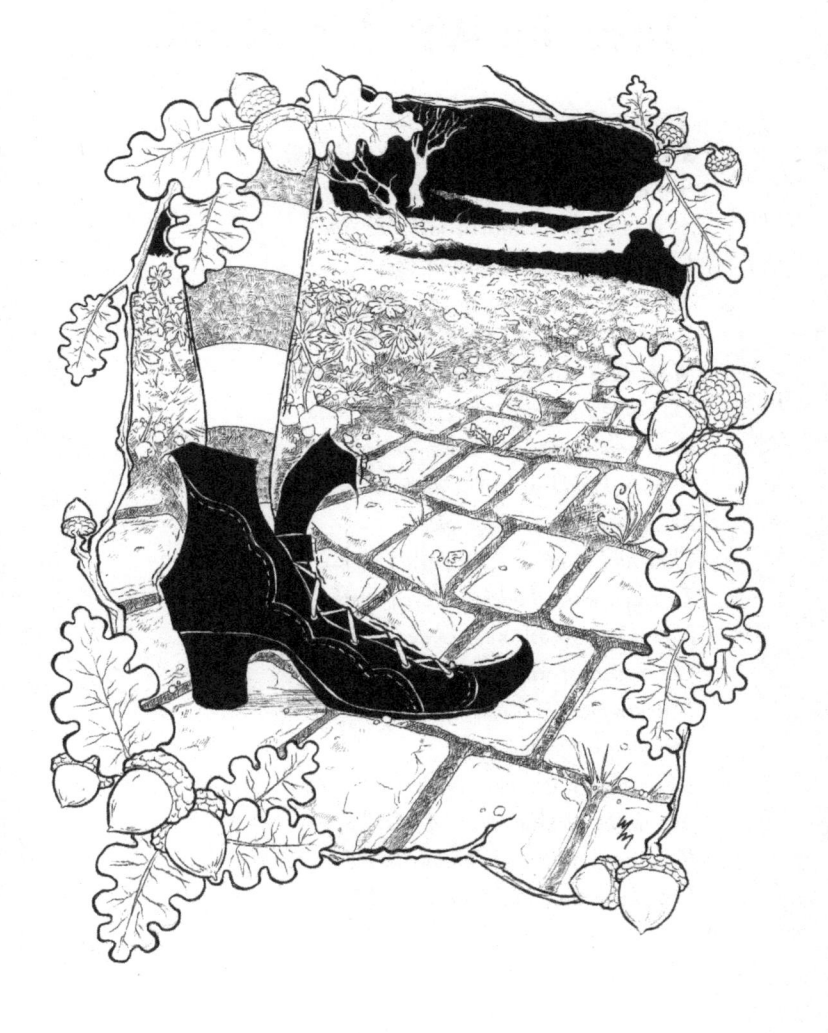

Into the Witch's Woods

*I*met a woman, young and fair.
Or was she haggard with wintered hair?
She had a magic by her side,
As autumn winds moved with her stride.
I asked her how like her to be,
And these are the words she said to me:
"Into the woods, find broken road,
Meet there with hare, raccoon, and toad.
On twisted broomstick, crown thy head,
By acorns capped on brown or red.
Be then knight of woven dreams,
As ones of fire past life glean.
Then find in circle a dragon's breath,
To reach where bodes not even death.
Now who's to say what came of me?
Can you trust what your eyes see?
Is it my face from afar?
Traveling on falling star?
Do I stand where fairies play,
Across the glass at dawn of May?
If the truth you want bestowed,
Into the woods, find broken road."

Chapter One
Aunt Brynelda's Magical Trowel

Good old Aunt Brynelda was never a witch with particularly high aspirations. She didn't look to the moon or reach for the stars. Quite the contrary, in fact. Aunt Brynelda was a witch who dug her fingers into the dirt. One who followed the humble path of the twiddling green. A garden witch. She loved to hum with the mosses, to trade with the blossoms, and to know the secrets of the roots and the woods.

Always keeping to herself, however, Aunt Brynelda was never more than a field mouse in the world beyond her hedges. Never known for more than a peep or a scurry as far as her distant neighbors were concerned. So,

there she knelt, grass stains on her apron, soil stains on her sleeves, her brown hair in a floppy bun, and her button nose brushing against the leaves of a heather shrub as she tended to her garden.

In her hand, she held a terrible old trowel. There was no telling where the rust ended and the dirt began. But she loved this trowel more than anything else in the world. It'd been with her through thick and thin and thumb on thorn—a gift from her mother. Her mother had received it from her uncle, and he from his grandmother, and she from her father or sister or sister's baker; who could keep track? But the trowel had survived the darkest depths and the thickest brambles. So, with it, Aunt Brynelda knew that whatever came, she would be able to face it.

As her luck would have it, this would be tested much sooner than expected. Aunt Brynelda was quietly humming to herself and her rooted friends, preening away at her proud shrub, when suddenly from behind her:

"What lovely flowers," an uneven voice croaked.

Aunt Brynelda jumped as if stung by a bee and squeaked in surprise. Her hair would have been standing on end if it wasn't already knotted into a bun. Turning around, she saw a gammer, a decrepit old country woman, peering wide-eyed at Aunt Brynelda's heathers. She had craggy tanned skin, gray hair adorned with mismatched braids, and a dress which seemed to have once been a beautiful peasant's gown but was now tattered and darkened with age. She stood with hard, clunky shoes upon a patch of mint, crushing the leaves.

The garden witch wanted to shoo the old gammer to save her poor patch of mint. But it had been so long since she had talked to anyone who wasn't sprouting from soil, the words choked in her throat.

"Are these flowers yours?" the gammer warbled, ruining her way over the rest of the patch towards the heathers.

"Well, they..." Aunt Brynelda managed to peep before the old woman began snapping the heathers from the shrub, placing them between her braids and upon the ancient lace of her dress, arranging others into a bouquet.

"Aren't they lovely...?" the old woman lilted as she slowly poised and twirled. "Though I've journeyed and searched, never a heather as lovely as this." Aunt Brynelda fidgeted, unsure what to do. The gammer smiled and trounced her way back over the mint with her hard, clunky shoes, spilling heather blossoms as she went.

The witch hurried to her once beautiful, now balding shrub. She gently caressed the plant, as if tending a wound. Then, with haste, she gripped her trowel, touched it to her heart, kissed the blade twice, and plunged it into the earth by the shrub. Shutting her hazel eyes tightly, she murmured:

> *"Sprig to heal,*
> *Petal to feel,*
> *Root dig deep, and seed reveal."*

She chanted these words until she hardly had any breath left in her. Then, opening her latched eyes again, she saw before her that the shrub had once again begun to bud. With a sigh of relief and a grateful smile, the witch pulled the trowel out from the earth and lovingly brushed off the dirt. Turning to her mint patches next, she wore a brief look of weariness but replaced it quickly with determination, repeating the spell on the patch until the leaves were vibrant and whole again.

Exhausted beneath a sun which had begun to set, Aunt Brynelda stumbled her way back into her ivy-covered cottage. Kicking off her shoes and removing her dirty apron, she barely managed to let her hair down before falling face-first into her fluffy bed and drifting away into a deep sleep.

The next day, Aunt Brynelda peeled herself away from her pillow with great difficulty. She felt like a beetle on the bottom of a shoe. Wobbling her way out of bed, she set about her morning routine, hoping with all hope that her next step wouldn't stumble out from under her. Finally, after washing and changing her clothes—and miraculously not finding herself face-first on the floorboards—she picked up her trusty trowel and set out into her garden. Her troubles practically fell out of her body upon seeing that her heather shrub had regrown all of its flowers; it looked as beautiful as ever in the morning sun.

Not too shabby, Brynelda, she thought to herself behind a smirk. Bunching together her tawny skirts, she slowly knelt towards a zucchini patch that was just beginning to ripen. Of course, it wasn't long after she drew forth her trowel that the hedges were once again crossed. A large boar this time stood, casting a shadow over the garden. It looked about, sweeping the land with its eyes as if searching for vermin. A huffy snort left its mouth upon spotting Aunt Brynelda timidly staring back at it. She feared the boar would charge at her, and the poor witch had barely enough strength at the moment to sweat nervously, much less run for shelter.

The boar's beady eyes barely glinted at her, however. Aunt Brynelda turned her attention on the figure slowly approaching from behind it. It was the old gammer from the day before. This time, however, the gammer looked much less like a shriveled weed. Her back was straighter, her braids more elegant, her lips painted, her cheeks rouged, and her gown had gone from the shade of reused bloomers to that of a deep bluebell.

A smile was pasted to the gilded gammer's face as she made her way towards Aunt Brynelda. Her hard shoes crushed a yarrow bunch as she moved closer, holding out a fist filled with the cut heathers.

"They've wilted," she sighed in a clear voice. "I don't want them anymore." She dropped the heathers in front of the button-nosed witch, who watched them fall with pain.

The gammer then shifted her smiling gaze towards the zucchini growing at Aunt Brynelda's knees. "Ah. I'll take these."

Aunt Brynelda sharpened at this, opening her mouth as the gammer knelt down. "Oh! I... I'd rather you—" But Aunt Brynelda was cut off by the large boar shoving its way between the two. It pushed the witch away like an old stick, and she fell into the dirt, fraying her bun of hair.

The gammer stood up, wrenching the zucchini from the soil, taking a deep bite from its skin. Dirt coated her lips and teeth as she chewed with passionate delight.

"Though I've journeyed and searched, never a zucchini as delectable as this." She gave the witch a distant smile and walked in the direction from which she came, trampling over more herbs as she went, the boar in tow.

Aunt Brynelda shook her head with disbelief. After lifting herself up from the dirt, she sorrowfully looked about her garden. Swallowing the lump in her throat, the witch gathered her strength and her trowel once more. She touched the blade to her heart, kissed it twice, and plunged it into the barren zucchini patch. Clenching her eyes shut, she whispered:

"Sprig to heal,
Petal to feel,
Root dig deep, and seed reveal."

She repeated this again and again. Finally, when the witch felt sick from exhaustion, she ceased her chanting and opened her eyes. The patch had begun to sprout beautiful orange-yellow flowers. Aunt Brynelda smiled weakly, dabbing her forehead free of cold sweat. She could hardly keep her eyes open but still pulled herself heavily to her feet. She staggered back towards her cottage, a dry wheeze in the back of her throat. Then she toppled over onto her bed, only managing to remove her boots this time before plummeting into a deep, deep sleep.

The next morning, Aunt Brynelda slowly awoke. Her hazel eyes opened to a bloodshot slit, and every muscle upon her bones ached and trembled. After a time, she removed herself from her bed, trying desperately to tame her now matted hair. Caressing the trowel in her apron pocket in an effort to comfort herself, Aunt Brynelda peeked out her window to gaze upon her garden.

With great shock—but maybe not great disbelief at this point—she saw a large snake slithering its way through the beds of greenery. Then, to her right, the boar emerged, stomping over patches of vervain. In a heavy weakness but even heavier frustration, Aunt Brynelda furrowed her brow and pursed her lips, shooting her eyes here and there looking for that horrible old gammer.

As if with delight, the gammer rose up from just beyond the windowsill. Aunt Brynelda sprung back in surprise, tripping over herself and clattering to the floor. This time, the gammer was a sight of immense beauty. Her gray-streaked hair was twisted up into curls and fastened with elegant pins; her dress was now the color of rich honey, which matched her chains and bracelets and rings upon rings. Her teeth even glinted like the diamonds dotting her neck. "Hello, dear," the gilded gammer hummed, plucking a honeysuckle flower from the vine outside the window. "You don't look well. Perhaps you should rest more."

The witch huffed, working herself up to confront the gammer, but one step nearly landed the poor woman flat on her face. She gazed around the small cottage and spotted a rake leaning against the wall. Gingerly, she eased her way towards the item, using it to steady herself as she stood. Now determined, Aunt Brynelda limped outside, approaching the gammer.

Taking a deep breath, she stuttered, "Y-you need—"

"I need a bigger basket." The gammer smiled, holding a large wicker basket filled to the brim with flowers, herbs, fruits, and vegetables. "Though I've journeyed and searched, never a bouquet as full as this."

Aunt Brynelda stared at the basket, horrified, then around at her patches, which were now torn and ravaged. Her eyes met the gammer's. Tears began to well up, drowning the image. "You...you...." she tried in a tiny voice.

The snake and the boar slowly crept from their corners of the garden towards the two women.

"Yes?" The gammer smiled her pasted smile. She seemed to grow taller and fuller while the witch felt as if she were crumpling on the spot.

Suddenly, the snake shot up from behind her. It spiraled itself around Aunt Brynelda like a coil of lightning. Gasping, she fell to the ground. The snake circled around her neck and tightened its grip. She wheezed for breath; her ever-reddening eyes bulged from her head, streaming with tears.

The gammer slowly approached the struggling witch. She knelt down, wearing her pasted smile as she ever did. Reaching out her hand, she plucked a marigold by Aunt Brynelda's face and added it to her basket.

"Not long now, dear," she chimed as Aunt Brynelda wilted.

A Witch's Book of Terribles

Just as everything began to turn black, the small witch felt something hot in her apron. Whatever it was twitched and then bolted from its spot. Abruptly, the snaked hissed and unraveled itself. Aunt Brynelda gasped and coughed and sobbed all at once. Through blurry eyes, she looked up to see the gammer without her pasted smile for the first time as she looked in shock at the snake who was writhing before her. On its long body, Aunt Brynelda saw something stuck into its scales...

The trowel!

"You awful little witch!" the gammer howled. "Look what you've done!" She pulled the trowel away from the snake, throwing the instrument to the ground, then cooed at her pet to soothe its pain.

Aunt Brynelda slowly reached for her trowel, but before her fingers could brush its handle, a fat hoof came down over it, shattering the beloved tool. Aunt Brynelda yelped, looking up at the angry boar, its eyes like needles stabbing into her.

"Leave here!" the gammer shouted at the witch as she comforted the hurt snake. "Leave my garden!"

In a fearful hurry, Aunt Brynelda grabbed the shards of her trowel and heaved herself up with the rake. She stumbled as quick as she could from her garden. Flowers and leaves seemed to pull at her

skirts as she escaped beyond the hedges. Though she was tired, and weak, and soaked in sorrow, the witch didn't stop running. Not when she reached the woods, not when her mouth dried and her feet bled, not even when the sun gave way to the moon. It wasn't until the rake caught on a tree root and caused Aunt Brynelda to tumble onto the forest floor that she finally came to a still.

She lay there in the dirt for a long time, crying until her tears ran dry. She wasn't sure how long it had been. As far as she knew, the sun had come up and set again. Taking a shaky breath, Aunt Brynelda sat up. She looked around. The forest was dark, and she felt horribly alone. Menacing tree trunks with face-like knots stared out at her. Their sharp branches were like claws. Even cracks in the ground looked like hungry maws waiting to gobble her up. Suddenly, she felt horribly not alone, though wishing she still was.

She dug her hand into her apron pocket and pulled out the pieces of her trowel. She looked at them solemnly for a long moment. Finding an opening between the trees that was illuminated by a beam of moonlight, Aunt Brynelda crouched and dug a small hole. She touched the trowel pieces to her heart, kissed them twice, and buried them into the ground. She began to drift from consciousness, but as she did, she dreamily chanted:

> *"Sprig to heal,*
> *Petal to feel,*
> *Root dig deep, and seed reveal."*

Aunt Brynelda was awoken the next morning by a bright ray of sun. Its gold light filled her eyes as she eased them open. The forest was a blinding haze of warm white. As her sight adjusted, she could make out the trees, mosses of bright green, and bushels of leaves dancing overhead. The forest seemed to have changed overnight. And so had she. Her aches were gone, her health felt completely replenished, and a strength seemed to grow in her like a great oak.

Strangest of all, where Aunt Brynelda had set her trowel's grave, now grew a tall, noble tree. Sunlight bounced off its leaves like golden mirrors, and in its twisting bark, Aunt Brynelda swore she could see a face peering back at her. It comforted her, familiar somehow. That is until its wood parted at the mouth and spoke her name.

"*Ahh!*" she screeched, jolting up to her feet.

The tree chuckled and said, "Don't be afraid. You know me. I've been with you all your life, and longer still."

"Are...are you my trowel...?" Aunt Brynelda asked, barely managing to pull the sentence together.

"I was once your trowel. Now I am else-wise. Your love and your years have given me a rare magic. I have been reborn a spirit of the wood, now one with the lines of magic, to fuel the wonder in the world and those who would sustain it." The tree's warm, hollow eyes softened at Aunt Brynelda's fair confusion. "It is not meant to be understood, my dear witch. All that matters is you. Take your true strength and rise like the wild wood against those who would do you ill. Let none wilt you, let none consume you. Go now and sow the seeds of your victory."

"I'm...not sure..." Aunt Brynelda said, but the tree simply smiled patiently back at her. "Well, all right," she reluctantly agreed. She still had many more questions than she had sense, but the sprite's words inspired her. With a deep smile, she brushed the tree's face and felt it smile back.

Not yet sure of what she was going to do, Aunt Brynelda set off. Slowly at first, she tracked her way through the gold-lit forest. The claw-like branches from the night before now looked like friendly hands, leading her along the path. She gained confidence and haste. Her steps turned into a run, into a sprint. Her tawny, grass-stained skirts flew behind her, and her bun unraveled until her long brown hair sprawled around her like a mane of wild ivy.

She wasn't sure from where, but the words came to her like a river to the sea:

Aunt Brynelda's Magical Trowel

"With bramble, branch and thorn, I command thee—"

The earth beneath her seemed to move, speeding her through the forest paths as if she were the wind.

"By flora, stalk and spine, I set it free!"

The forest around her parted, making way for the witch. She could see her cottage blooming ever closer in the distance.

"Vine and burrow to the sky—"

The gammer ran out from the cottage, looking astonished and terrified at the fiery witch looming on writhing mounds of earth before her. Roots sprung up from the soil, capturing the old woman.

"Swallow thou who's time is nigh!"

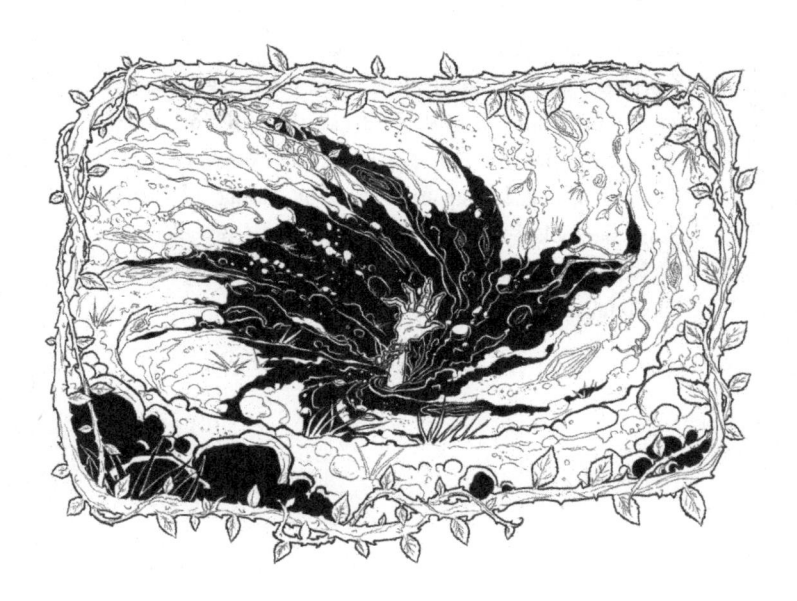

The ground thrashed upward around the gammer. Walls of soil surrounded her. Her rouged face turned pale white as she spun to search for an escape, but roots gripped tight to her bejeweled dress. The boar and the snake had rushed from the cottage, and seeing the power of Aunt Brynelda, abandoned their master, fleeing beyond the hedges.

"But..." escaped the gammer's lips in a pathetic whimper. Though before she could utter another word, the walls of soil crashed down upon her. The ground pulsed and swallowed her deeper and deeper as one would drink from a bottle. Only awe hung on the gammer's face as her gown dirtied, her hair clumped, and her jewels scattered. "But—" she uttered once more, and then she was gone.

The mounds of earth beneath Aunt Brynelda subsided. The cavernous patches of dirt seemed to mend themselves as the witch's feet walked by. Grasses regrew, herbs flourished, buds and sprouts bloomed, even her heather shrub glowed with new life. The garden seemed to cheer and dance with joy at the witch's return.

Tying her hair back into a bun, and walking with a newfound strength, Aunt Brynelda smiled at her rooted friends. Everything was well again. Better than before, even. Except for one little thing: a spiny weed had sprouted from where the gammer met her end. The witch knelt down and, with satisfaction, pulled it up from the root. Patting her hands clean, she looked around the garden and said proudly:

"Though I've journeyed and searched, never a garden as wonderful as this."

Are You a Witch?

If thou hold virtue of magic,
Beyond all reason, far past logic,
Thou who bears the crossroad's beat,
Who hearkens to its true entreat,
Thou be beckoned from stagnation,
Above the bonds of observation.
If thrice the corners call thy name,
And thrice you seek to stake your claim.
To master arts and ever spin,
In this round with wayward kin.
Then know in every fiber stitched,
You walk the path of a sure-born witch.

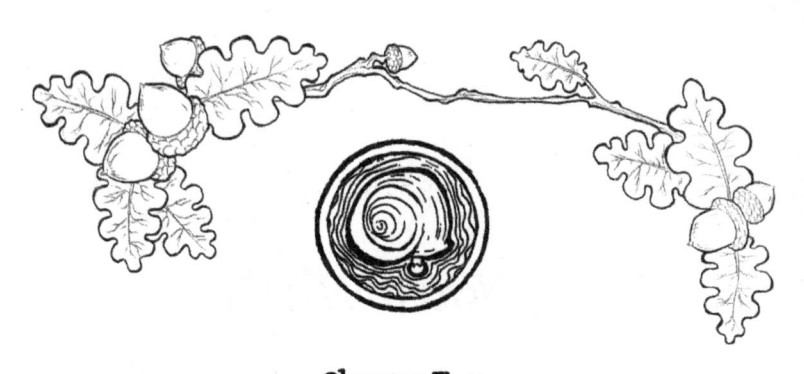

Chapter Two
Ipscingen of the Wishing Well

Ipscingen the Crafty, Ipscingen the Stalwart. Renowned in power and wit, a master of spell crafting, and awfully silver-tongued to boot, he was known for many wonderful things, for there was little that he wasn't wonderful at. One thing Ipscingen decidedly wasn't wonderful at, however, was watching where he was going to ensure he didn't fall into an old, dry well. He also happened to not be very talented at escaping said well.

"Unfortunate," he said to himself. "It was such a nice day too. If only the clouds and the birds hadn't been so distracting, I wouldn't find myself at the bottom of this awful hole."

He pulled off his pointy hat to scratch his head as he waited for an idea to come to him. He hopped around on his upcurved shoes and twiddled his curly red beard. Alas, no matter of scratch, hop, or twiddle would aid him in this plight. He'd call to his familiars for help...if he had his talismans. He'd rebuild the well's stones into stairs...if he could consult his sigils. But all he seemed to have was dirt. Not even weeds grew down in the well.

Fortunately, Ipscingen had an almost otherworldly sense of instinct. An instinct which told him that everything would turn out just fine. In fact, he felt so sure of this that he decided to simply sit and wait. The next thing he felt, however, was less pleasant.

"Ow!" he yelped as a coin dropped onto his spiky rust-colored hair. Putting his hat back on, he looked up to see why the forecast had suddenly called for pocket change.

"Oh?" a voice with a thick boorish accent came from the opening of the well. A woman with straw-like hair and a long nose peered over the edge. "What are ya doin' in the wishing well? Tryin' to steal people's coins?" she scolded.

"No, I fell in and can't climb my way out. Could you help me?"

"Fell in, didja...? Unlikely." She leaned closer and took a long, hard look at Ipscingen. Spying his pointed hat, she perked up. "You're the witch of this well! Aren't ya? Can ya grant wishes?"

Proud of his great talents, Ipscingen was never one to make way for modesty. "I can!" he chuffed.

"If ya grant me one wish, I'll free ya from this well."

Ipscingen was a little wary of this, but agreed nonetheless. "What do you wish for?"

"There's a man in my village with feet as large as paddle oars and who's nearly twice the height of my house's doorway. His name is Edward. I've fallen in love with him and want to make him mine."

The witch contemplated this, then smiled. "Bring to me hair from his lapel, the unswung tongue of an iron-made bell, a spoon's worth of honey, measured with care, and a handkerchief pale as your breasts' skin is fair."

With a mildly annoyed sigh, the woman disappeared from view. After some time, she returned, carrying with her a small brown bag. "Mr. Witch in the Well! I have the things to craft your spell!" She placed the bag into a bucket at the crown of the well, lowered it down to Ipscingen, and then quickly reeled the bucket back up when he collected the bag.

"Ah, yes. These will do," he nodded, looking over the ingredients. Ipscingen placed the bell's tongue to his side. He then dolloped some of the honey onto the corner of the handkerchief and pressed the strands of hair into it. He folded the corner over and added another dollop. He continued this while humming to himself:

> *"Cloth the shade of heart's true passion,*
> *Ever folded, ever more,*
> *With honey, sweet, do I fasten,*
> *To attend and to adore."*

"Is it done?" the woman squinted from behind her long nose.

"His love is yours. Whenever he lays his eyes upon you, his heart will swell."

"Wonderful," she swooned.

"Will you help me out of this well?"

"I'll need to make certain it's worked first," she said curtly, stepping away from the opening.

Ipscingen sighed and leaned back against the well. Time passed, and the woman returned with a smile stretched clear across her face.

"It worked!" she cheered.

"Naturally." Ipscingen smirked. "Will you help me out of this well, now?"

"One more wish and I promise I will!" she huffed.

Ipscingen narrowed his eyes and tapped his curved shoes impatiently. "What is it now?"

"I have a reputation as somewhat of a tippler around town, and now Edward's friends won't bless our love. I need my reputation cleared."

Ipscingen rolled his eyes and thought for a minute, then said, "Bring me a bottle you've emptied in spate, the dust from a stoop of someone you hate, to rosemary whispered a secret you tell, and a mirror that fits within my palm's ell."

The woman rushed off without a second thought and returned in half the time she had before. "Mr. Witch in the Well! I have the things to craft your spell!" She lowered the ingredients down to Ipscingen in the well's bucket. The bucket was then quickly reeled back up as she peered eagerly into the well to watch his work.

Ipscingen placed the mirror to his side. He crumbled the rosemary and combined it with the dust into the bottle. He thricely tapped the bottle's mouth to the space between his bushy eyebrows and chanted:

> *"Let them forget and shame be naught,*
> *Be hazy,*
> *Be lazy,*
> *Ignore before.*
> *Heed in their mind is lost on the spot.*
> *No prattle,*
> *No tattle,*
> *No slander no more."*

He spilled the contents out from the bottle into the dirt at his feet and looked back up to the woman. "They remember nothing of your reputation now, my dear lady. All shall look upon you as a stranger."

The long-nosed woman squealed in excitement. "Fantastic! Once I'm sure it's worked, I'll return for ya." She adjusted her shawl and turned on her toe, away from the well. Ipscingen slumped over in disappointment.

Soon after, the woman returned, skipping and singing. "It worked!" she giggled down the well. "No one even threw me a sideways glance! Edward and I are gonna marry in no time!"

"So...will—"

"Not so fast!" the woman scoffed, flipping back her stringy hair and looking down her nose at Ipscingen in overlording annoyance. "I'll be needin' one last thing 'fore I can let ya out of this well. Edward and I will need quite the estate 'fore we can marry. He *is* very tall after all. Ya can't expect us both to squeeze into a tiny shack, can ya? Cast a spell to grant us exuberant wealth!"

Ipscingen furrowed his eyebrows and crossed his arms at the awful woman. Yet, after a time of thought, he said, "bring me a hermit crab's barren shell, the nut from a tree which recently fell, a discarded coin from a place of commotion, and wax from a candle, lit in devotion."

The woman clapped her hands excitedly and pranced off. In no time, she had come back. "Mr. Witch in the Well! I have the things to craft your spell." Lowering the ingredients down to Ipscingen, she leaned over the well to watch the witch grant her another wish.

He first placed the crab's shell to his side. Then he buried the nut into the well's dirt. Over this, he placed the wax and began making hatches and Xs into it with the coin while chanting:

"From this place with Xs mark,
Treasure take the hunter's hark.
When from this spot, thou doth embark,
To find thy bounty in the dark."

"Where's my money?" the woman asked eagerly.

Ipscingen straightened himself up to address the woman. "Leaving from this well, the seeker will find treasure readily revealed to them in whatever direction they take. Now, will you help me escape from here?"

The woman sighed in frustration and spoke slowly. "Ya know I can't do that until I see that your spell has worked, witch. Then I will set ya free. Unless I find another need for your talents."

"If you insist," Ipscingen shrugged, "but it is my advice that you free me now or fall into regret."

The woman scoffed at Ipscingen and laughed. "Ya threatenin' me, well-witch? I hold all the cards here. You'll be free when and *if* I decide." With that, she threw her shawl over her shoulder and set off to find her treasure.

Ipscingen shook his head and smiled mischievously, tsking the woman's arrogance. He knelt down and took from his side the unrung tongue of an iron-made bell, the mirror that fits within his palm's ell, and the hermit crab's barren shell. With a long hair from his curly red beard, he attached the tongue to the inside of the shell and rattled it thrice. It chimed an eerie sound as he placed the shell upon the mirror. Pricking his finger with his sharpest tooth, he then produced a drop of blood onto the shell. He took the mirror into his palm and spoke these words:

> *"One, two, three let ring,*
> *With blood upon, I'm given way.*
> *One, two, three I bring,*
> *Thou instead to take my stay.*
> *For she doth the death bell knell,*
> *To bind her down the bone-dry well."*

Ipscingen's eyes were flooded with light as he stood in full sunshine at the mouth of the well. A proud smile etched across his face. But it wasn't long at all before he heard a shrill shriek from down the cobblestone hole.

"I warned you," Ipscingen called, looking into the well with a shrug.

"*No!*" the woman howled. "Ya won't get away with this! My love, Edward, will come for me!"

"'Whenever he lays his eyes upon you, his heart will swell,'" Ipscingen recited, "but he can't lay his eyes upon you when you're trapped in a well, now can he?"

"Oh, no! My Edward! Well...someone will notice I'm gone! They'll come for me!"

"'All shall look upon you as a stranger.' How can someone notice you're missing if they can't even remember you?"

"But...but my treasure? At the very least, *it* waits for me!"

"'Leaving from this well, the seeker will find treasure readily revealed to them in whatever direction they take.'" Ipscingen straightened his pointed hat, and unruffled his coat. "So, if you don't mind, I have a treasure to find." With that, Ipscingen turned away from the woman's dumbfounded expression and promptly set off for a very lucrative afternoon.

The Ballad of Culfom Crau

A *witch who wards is very wise in magic and in measure,*
To keep at bay,
What could betray,
And safeguard all they treasure.
One such fellow known for this, he goes by Culfom Crau,
His wards are true,
And clever too,
They hold poise even now.
It didn't matter what may come, or how, or when, or why,
Spells dropped dead,
Then villains fled,
Each as they came by.
Yet Culfom Crau, in all his pride, would often boast and
brag,
When one dim day,
You'd hear him say,
To Cairlock of the Crag:
"I have bested every foe, and you're no better man.
I've swayed steel,
And made storms kneel,
So catch me if you can."
Well, Cairlock isn't known for wits, nor is he one to shout.
With one firm thrust,
His fist was just,
And took the great witch out.
Then with that hit, Crau hit the road and left his resigna-
tion.
Thus Culfom Crau,
He learned just how,
A ward heeds invitation.

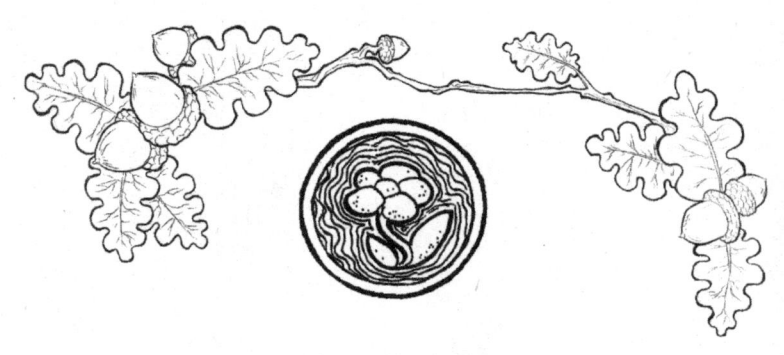

Chapter Three
Ditty Denna and the Dismal Duenna

The night was fearsome as the howling winds crackled with an ice-like cold. Above, the sky seemed to stretch forever. In its center was adorned a large, round moon glowing with pearly light. Thin clouds spiraled around it as if falling into its depths. It was an ominous night. A powerful night. It was a night for casting.

The witches sat huddled together, shadows against light, appearing to any passerby as a gaggle of dark figures in a brightly lit window. A window which shone from the highest room of the old Gothic house at the end of the street. But although the figures may have painted the picture of a group of menacing hags, they were, in fact, five little girls giggling on a bed. Each one was taller than the last, with hair of varying lengths, all in the shade of onyx.

"Let's do this one!" cried one girl, holding up a small leather-bound book and pointing to a passage marked "For Sunny Days."

"Not that one," said the tallest girl. "We'd need a red chili for it, and we're all out."

"This one!" squealed another, pulling open a page titled "To Speak with a Cat" from a long, thin tome.

"No, we can only do that one when the moon is still waxing," replied the tallest.

Diddy Denna and the Dismal Duenna

"Oh!" One girl holding a dusty pink journal perked up, gesturing to swirly letters that read "Change All Flavors to Sweet."

"This says we need pink and cream-colored candles," the tall girl sighed. "We only have ivory."

"Well..." a small voice chimed from the corner of the room, "maybe you can do something...different?"

All five girls begrudgingly turned their onyx heads towards the corner. Another girl stared back at them through wide gray eyes. She was smaller than the rest, mottled with freckles all along her tiny frame, with long marmalade-colored hair tied into loops on the sides of her head.

"That's not how it works, Denna," one girl said, rolling her eyes.

"Magic isn't just something you can *make up*," sighed another.

The tallest girl sat up and sneered at Denna. "These spells have years and years of witchcraft behind them. They aren't like one of your ridiculous little *ditties*. They *mean* something."

"But—" Denna began.

"This one!" a pig-tailed girl cried in excitement. She held an ancient manuscript with pages that looked so old they almost had the texture of tree bark. On it, she pointed to a spell titled "A Call to the Faerie."

The tall girl looked over the page, her eyes widening in excitement the more she read. "Mystical faerie...knows the secrets of every written spell...able to lift the spirits of her chosen few...yes!" she exclaimed. "This is perfect!"

"What is it...?" Denna peeped curiously, moving from her bed.

"No, Denna," one of the girls scoffed, getting up to escort Denna out of the room. "You stay in the hall and watch out for mother and father. They'd be furious if they knew we were playing with the spell books."

"But I want to do magic too!" Denna pouted.

"Then make up another little ditty, Denna!" called a different girl from the group.

Denna frowned at the closing door and sounds of laughter from her sisters. She dropped to the floor with her arms crossed, her eyes squinted in frustration.

"My magic does too work!" she mumbled to herself. "It's just different." She sat for a moment, steaming, then softened. She began to hum a tune to herself and trace spirals, swirls, and shapes into the air—ones that only she could see. As she did so, she sang:

"Bibblin, bubblin', trelum coppit! Wimitty tim tum teller hop it! Fresh-baked bread and butterflies. Frog's legs and a fun surprise."

As she sang, her spirals began to ripple the air. Her words were sung back to her as the rippling air formed into a shape. As if looking into a mirror, Denna saw her own body form in front of her.

It was far from the first time this had occurred. She had no idea what she was doing, or how, but when you're as lonely as Denna was, all company is good company—even

if that company can only be more of yourself. The doubled girls smiled at each other as they sang. The walls changed colors from an aged yellow to hues of bright pinks and blues. Sparkles filled the air, and candy fell like raindrops from the ceiling. It was like jumping into a dream of her own making. But Denna was quickly pulled back into reality by a sharp push from behind. Her dream world vanished like a snuffed-out candle flame, turning back into the narrow hallway she was so used to.

"Don't sit in front of the door, Denna!" one of the sisters ordered as she quietly hurried on her tiptoes down the hall. More of her sisters followed, returning after a time with arms full of flowers, kitchen supplies, candles, paints, and other various items. When they all returned, the tallest sister looked at Denna and gave her a wink before closing the door again in her face.

I hope they summon a big, ugly spider, Denna thought crossly.

The five girls stood in their room, spaced evenly amongst a ring of honey-warm candlelight and fresh flowers. They had pretty symbols painted on their cheeks and had dressed the door and windows with white sheets. The middle sister whose hair reached her elbows approached the center of the circle with a milk-filled bowl and placed it down.

"Are these all the items?"

The tallest girl held the ancient grimoire, listing the tools of the spell. "Ivory sheets upon thresholds, sigils of the faerie, freshly picked blossoms, unburnt tapers, sweetened cream, a lemon, and..." she looked up nervously. The girls looked nervously back at her. "Blood upon a virgin kiss."

"Do we have to?" whined the girl with the shortest hair.

The tallest thought for a moment, brushing her fringe from her face. Then she straightened herself sternly and looked at her sisters. "Well, do you want to see a faerie or not?" With that, she bit down on her lip, wincing slightly as a line of blood produced itself.

The rest of the sisters traded glances, then trying to muster up the same resolve, they began chewing their lips. Some were able to draw blood on the first few tries. The others took longer as they gnawed away at tender flesh, until finally each sister's mouth was stained with red. The tallest nodded. She took up the lemon and kissed it, leaving a small red mark. She passed it along to her sisters, who all did the same.

When the lemon was dotted with each of their kisses, they set it into the bowl. Each sister stood in place, staring at the bowl, not letting a single breath escape in anticipation. Unfortunately, the lemon simply bobbed over the cream. Slumping her shoulders in disappointment, the tallest sister opened her mouth to speak, but just as she did, the lemon dropped to the bottom of the bowl, swallowed by white. Smiles streaked across the sisters' faces like lightning as they squirmed giddily.

But their joy froze when the candleflames shifted from their warm glows to a sickly oyster green. The milk began to curdle, cracking like an aged painting, as the perfume of flowers around them turned rancid and stale.

"Something's wrong!" one of the girls cried.

"We need to stop the spell!"

They tried to move, but their feet were like stone, and with each attempt the skin beneath their painted cheeks tightened. Hopelessly, they all looked to the tallest sister. Her eyes darted to each one of them, attempting to give comforting words or instructions. However, unable to conjure a single helpful thought, she could only sputter out syllables in response to their pleading faces.

Suddenly, the sheets on the thresholds began to thrash, as if something behind them was trying to get in. The candleflames flickered violently, too, making even the shadows themselves seem fearful of what was about to happen. The smallest of the five screamed. Then the rest followed suit.

The curdling milk was as thick as clay now. The bowl started to spin, and then, like a bubble, the milk popped. The flames extinguished. The sheets hung as stiff as boards. Even the girls went silent, tears streaming down their spellbound cheeks. Chunks of sour and sweet speckled the dark room.

Each sister was too scared to speak. The sounds of their breathing bounced off the walls. Blackness filled the room nearly as much as rancid stench. They tried to make out something. Anything. A sliver of light from the full moon outside crept its way through the sheets, but it wasn't enough. Maybe they could figure out each other's shadows. All six of them seemed to be still as death itself. The worst part, however, was that there shouldn't have been six of them.

From the bowl in the center emanated the familiar gray-green light from before. A dark figure stood hunched over the glow. Slowly, it rose to its full height. It was a woman. She was impossibly thin with a long, gaunt face, a hairless brow, and ice-white lips which were spotted with a red liquid. Both her blanched dress and long, dark hair, although thin, looked heavier than they should. They seemed dry to the touch but hung as if wet.

She gazed about at the girls with a stern expression on her face. A gray silk-like substance slowly bloomed from her back. It rose like a pair of wings, but then thumped hard onto the floor the more it grew. It spread out from behind her, coating the circle. As the girls whimpered and tried again to move, the substance crept up their bodies. They screamed. Louder than before. They struggled fiercely to be free, the substance reaching up to some of their shoulders by now. The skin beneath their painted symbols was turning red and concave from how hard it was tightening on them.

"Now, now..." the faerie spoke in a slow, deep voice. "Little girls must not stray. Let Dismal Duenna show you the way."

Denna had been pounding on the door for what seemed like ages. Not long after, her mother and father had raced to the door as well, attempting to open it with spells, potions, talismans, and even brute force. But the Duenna's magic convicted them to powerlessly listen to the girls' wails—until finally, their screams stopped, and the three witches were finally able to break through the barrier.

They fell forward in full force, being met first with a white sheet, and second with an unearthly stench. Frantically, the mother and father tore away at the sheet covering them, calling out their daughters' names. The adults managed to free themselves from the sheet, and as it fell from their eyes, Denna heard their yells grow silent as her heartbeat grew louder. Once the sheet passed her eyes, and her vision changed from a scene of white to a dark, stained room, she could see why they froze in silence.

The faerie was gone, and so were her five sisters. All that lay in their place were bundles of rotting flowers, chunks of curdled milk, and five onyx-haired corpses.

There was no funeral. Votives were not lit, wild violets did not adorn their pillows, and dandelion roots were not worn in reverence. Even a period of mourning did not fall upon that old Gothic house. There simply wasn't time. Not when the dead needed to be risen.

Denna's mother and father tucked themselves away into the stregareum where the family kept all their magical tomes and ingredients. They formed talismans from scrolls of wood, knotted twine and crossed iron around balls of wax, and placed heavy enchantments upon kettles, chains, and boxes. In fact, it seemed that as they skimmed through the large family grimoire, there wasn't a spell they didn't prepare.

Denna, on the other hand, was feeling lonelier than ever. She sang her ditties much more frequently now. Her second self was good enough company. She always seemed much brighter and happier than Denna was lately, as were the dancing roses and talking animals she sang into the world around her. For a short time, she was content. That is until her contentment crumbled hard with her magical world as a familiar smell filled her with dread.

A sour sweetness filled the halls of the Gothic house. Without thought, Denna's feet moved from under her; she ran straight to the stregareum, where the stench was the strongest. She could see a sickly green light shining from beneath the door. Inching closer with every fear-choked breath, Denna managed to crack open the door just enough to see inside the room, past a stiff white sheet.

Her eyes teared up from the stinging smell, and it took a while for her vision to adjust, but once it did, she could see the figure of a terrible, hollow woman in the center of the room. Flanking both sides of her were two tall human shapes, tightly wrapped in some kind of smoke-like fabric that flowed from the woman.

"There is no spell written that I do not know," the faerie seemed to laugh through an expressionless face as she addressed the figures. "It was futile to think me unprepared."

The strange material retreated back into her body, and just as it did, the bodies of Denna's parents dropped to the floor. Denna gasped in surprise before she could silence herself. It was over. First, it had taken her sisters. Now her

parents. All that was left was Denna and a wicked faerie who did not seem deaf to Denna's surprise. Her head slowly turned toward the door, and a frown spread across her white lips.

"Little girls must not stray. Let Dismal Duenna show you the way," the faerie lilted as she moved to the door. Her feet didn't move, but she slowly glided closer and closer as her heavy, black dress dragged over the floor.

Denna was fear-stricken. She didn't know what else to do. She took in a deep breath and gathered her strength.

To the Dismal Duenna's surprise, the door opened just wide enough for a small, ginger-haired girl to squeeze through. She stood defiantly against the faerie, beaming with an unseen fire.

The faerie furrowed her hairless brow into a stern, disapproving expression. "No, no, little child. Make not such a face. Your crudeness, your rebelliousness. I shall soon free you of these...."

With that, the substance bloomed once again from the faerie's back. It fell hard upon the floor, blanketed itself around the room, and twisted up Denna's body. Her eyes burned fiercely before finally being swallowed too by the substance. The Duenna wore a look of satisfaction, but it was quickly replaced by confusion. The substance slightly loosened enough for the faerie to look inside. She peered closely at it, then pulled it away more forcefully like a magician would a tablecloth.

Denna was gone. Truly gone. Not even a corpse was sprawled in her place. The Dismal Duenna was furious, and now through gritted teeth, she repeated: "Little...girls...must not...stray. Let...Dismal Duenna...show you...the way."

She began to search the stregareum, gliding over the floorboards. But not a moment after she began did a big, blue, sugar-coated flower sprout from the faerie's shoulder.

She shot a disgusted look at the blossom. "What manner of magic is this?"

The Dismal Duenna tore at the flower, and once she did, it poofed into a plume of sugar. And where each grain fell, another flower grew in its place. "*What?* What is—this childish nonsense must cease!" The Duenna's already paper-thin patience was growing thinner as her bony fingers tried to rid herself of this candy curse, to no avail.

Then, she froze. Her glassy eyes bulged, as did her gaunt face. Her hovering feet dropped to the floor, and with a heave, she wretched. Nothing seemed to exit her mouth; however, a deep gasp soon rose from the nearby body of Denna's mother. She opened her eyes and lifted her head to the scene. A second wretch from the faerie, and Denna's father did the same. Both parents stared dumbfounded at the creature before them as she wretched five more times.

As the Duenna writhed weakly on the floor, trying to gain her bearings, the door to the stregareum opened to a small, freckled girl singing a whimsical tune:

> *"Emtillory crillory lolly and cream,*
> *Buttercup flutter up and biddy bo beem."*

"Denna—!" her mother began, but she went mute when five more girls with onyx hair came through the door behind Denna and sang:

> *"Emtillory crillory lolly and cream,*
> *Buttercup flutter up and biddy bo beem."*

The faerie screeched on the floor, curled up into a ball and looking more like a sugar-coated shrub at this point as more and more flowers bloomed. The two parents looked at themselves in disbelief, tears welling in their eyes. With quivering smiles, they stood and joined their daughters in singing:

> *"Emtillory crillory lolly and cream,*
> *Buttercup flutter up and biddy bo beem."*

The Dismal Duenna's terrible screams were drowned out by the joyful tunes of the witches' song. More and more flowers filled her space. They bloomed bigger and bigger, until suddenly, *pop!* In a large flurry of sugar, the Dismal Duenna was gone. The room sparkled with sweet, and the witches' song stopped.

It was silent for a few moments, and then all at once, they pounced each other into a warm, tear-soaked embrace. Crying and laughing blended together as they hugged. Denna opened her eyes, and from over her sisters' shoulders, she saw a proud image of herself staring back at her. Denna nodded at her other self through her tears, and the spirit returned the nod before shimmering away with a gentle hum. Denna smiled and lost herself again in her family's huddle.

The Stregareum

The witches cast on stone and gale,
 Yet nary is their craft most able,
Than in the stead from which they hail,
Lit by flame and draped in sable.
Here at the place 'twixt dusk and dawn,
Where spirit, god, and fairy come,
The witch will claim their haven drawn,
Away to their Stregareum.

Chapter Four

The Lackadaisical Hare

The small village of Bosbury sat in a somewhat secluded part of the world. Comfortably nestled between a fishing shore and a dense forest, its rustic homes and cobblestone roads housed some interesting characters. Here, it wasn't unusual to find those who would speak to the trees or bicker over who gets to decide on the day's weather. This was a village of witches. Although not everyone was of a magical virtue, those who weren't and those who were lived in happy acceptance of each other, and the practice of magic flourished like any other skill; farming and bookkeeping went alongside divination and enchantments.

Among the village's occupants was a young boy named Pridge. Now, Pridge had been a witch since the day he was born. He was full of bristling magical power; of this he was certain. That power had yet to be accessed, but he was sure it would come in time. If it wasn't a grand planetary alignment or some ancient relic that would unlock his vast potential, then surely it would happen once he met his witch's familiar.

A witch's familiar is a spirit companion—often coming in the form of an animal—that creates a partnership with the witch in question. The witch offers care, food, and other experiences of the material world, while the familiar in turn teaches valuable secrets of magical ways. For the witches of

Bosbury, there was no greater honor than to be granted their familiars. Well, for *most* of the witches that rang true. For Pridge, the process was taking far too long and becoming rather cumbersome—especially for a witch with a destiny as great as his.

"Two tibias crossed..." Pridge said to himself as he looked over a small grouping of bones before him through half-open pewter-blue eyes. "It looks like I'm not going out today." With that, the boy made his decision and laid back down across his soft couch.

Now, it wasn't that Pridge was completely incompetent in his current state. He often had dreams of a prophetic nature and was able to read bones to near exact accuracy. Not to mention he was clever. If anything, Pridge was clever. As impressive as this would sound to a mundane onlooker, however, it had become ever apparent to Pridge that he had fallen behind his peers.

A Witch's Book of Terribles

The custom among the witches here was that once every child turned thirteen, they would wait for the shore tides to reach the great holed stone. At that point, each young witch would need to walk the crooked path deep into the woods until they found the ancient oak with the face of a man. It was an old custom, often thought of as odd or even silly to the prosy-folk of Bosbury. To the witches, though, this was an essential part of one's training. It was from the Oaken Wight, after all, that the witches would attain their familiars.

Well, Pridge had turned thirteen over two months ago, attended five gatherings, and tripped seven times on the way down the rustic path. All this and he still hadn't attained his familiar. Many of the others already had theirs. He could see Artemisia with her yellow bird stirring up potions, and Jasper summoning small fires with his black dog. Yet, as exceptional as he was, Pridge still hadn't been given his. It was becoming clear to him that the Oaken Wight was not the answer to unlocking his powers, and thus, not worth his precious time.

This well-thought-out decision, however, was short-lived, as a man with heavily arched eyebrows and full charcoal hair—the same color as Pridge's—came to the doorway. A curious-looking stoat scurried about at his feet.

"Pridgemus Knock, what are you doing lollygagging about? The gatherings have begun!"

"The bones—" Pridge began to drawl, but he was cut off.

"If you're about to say anything other than the bones in your legs are broken, then you better hop to it and get yourself down that crooked path!" The man's eyebrows seemed to be arching even further the longer he talked. "Your grandmothers will be turning in their graves when they hear how you've been acting."

At that, Pridge begrudgingly dressed in his dark green suit and a pointed hood, then set off down the crooked path. He stopped occasionally along the way, picking berries to eat and veering slightly from the path to warm himself in the sun. It wasn't an easy path to walk, and he didn't often like doing it. Pridge wished each time he had to walk down this way that he could just be at the end of it.

Finally, Pridge reached the old oak—much later, it seemed, than everyone else. Little witches were all gathered around it, some sitting with their eyes closed in what looked like quiet conversation. Others were leaving cakes and powders or burning incenses that filled the air with a sweet fog. None of them paid him any attention as they were each going about their business trying to appease the Oaken Wight.

Pridge sat down by the tree, crossing his legs and looking at the others around him. He met the gaze of a braided girl who just raised her eyebrows at him as if to both tell him off for being late and mock him for coming at all.

Pridge just sneered back at her. She closed her eyes to commune with the Wight. Pridge, not wanting to look awkward, did the same.

He didn't hear any voices or sense a spirit at his side. Nevertheless, the witch boy made good use of this time imagining the great creature that would be his familiar.

With power like his, surely Pridge would receive a lion or a strong horse. Maybe even a dragon. His mind danced with these visions; they hopped about in his thoughts until he found himself waking with a snort. He was lying on the ground, and the sun had long since set. Not only that, but he was the only one there.

"How rude," he mumbled to himself as he stood up. "No one had the decency to even wake me before they left." He snuck a quick glimpse at the face in the oak, who, Pridge felt, was also looking back at him with an almost eerie smile lit solely by subtle moonlight. Pridge felt a shiver go up his spine. He turned around and made his difficult journey back up the path.

As fate would have it, the path was not any easier to walk in the dark, but eventually, he made it home. The streets were lit by deep gold lantern light, which was a treat to his eyes in the dark blue night. His feet ached for his bed as he approached home, but upon reaching his front door, he could see, just barely, a small lump on the ground barring the threshold.

"You old stoat," he mumbled at the lump. "Dad make you wait outside for me?" Pridge had utterly no time for pleasantries. So, he stomped past the old lump and into the house, leaving the door open just a crack for the animal. He made his way to his bed, and before his head could hit the pillow, he was asleep.

That night, the young witch had a dream where he was spoken to by a formless voice. The voice told him to brew a magic elixir which would awaken his hidden potential. For this elixir, he would need three things: a sun-bleached bone as white as salt, lace woven from milkweed thread, and the water which drowns a fallen star.

Throughout this dream, Pridge could feel a weight on his chest. It was warm and soft and occasionally itchy. His eyes slowly creaked open and blurry light streamed in through his eyelids. As the light became clearer, so did the revelation that the weight he felt on his chest wasn't just the feeling of his heart in a moment of dreamy mysticism.

Sitting on his chest, an old wood-colored hare stared at Pridge through an unmistakably bored expression. Understandably, this was met with a great deal of surprise as Pridge scrambled away from his bed. A mess of boy and blankets fell in one direction, and a strange hare in the other. The hare, however, seemed wholly unphased by this ordeal. Pridge looked over the edge of the bed to watch it laying in a heap of pillows. It stretched and sighed as if trying to muster up the strength to wake from a nap.

"You...you're my familiar?" Pridge began. The hare stared at him through a yawn and gave the young witch a quick nod. "I wasn't expecting a hare."

"You were expecting a dragon?"

"Well, yes! Or a lion. I'm not too picky."

The hare gave the boy a slight shrug.

"But a hare is nice too. As long as you can really make me powerful, I guess it doesn't matter what you look like."

At this, the hare gave its first glimpse of emotion. It was slight, but its eyes seemed to spark with an almost sly glint as its ears perked up slightly. "Then I suppose we shall begin."

The hare took Pridge—or rather, Pridge had taken the hare into his arms as it gave him poorly explained directions—to a small glade in the woods. Pridge found an old fallen tree to rest on as he waited for the hare to give him his next set of instructions. Instead, his familiar hopped over to a flat stone in the sunny center of the grass and curled itself up into a nap.

"Hey!" Pridge said, jumping up from the log. The hare lazily lifted its head and wiggled its nose at the flabbergasted witch. "Don't fall asleep! I took you out here so that you could unlock my great powers!"

"Yes, yes..." the hare yawned. "The first thing you'll need to do is retrieve a sun-bleached bone as white as salt."

"Where am I supposed to find one of those?"

The hare turned its heavy head towards the dense woods. "Look," it said, staring past the trees.

Pridge squinted his eyes and looked in the direction that the hare was motioning. Beyond the glade, just hidden in shadow, he saw a large figure sprawled across the ground. Pridge moved closer to see what it was, and once he did, he jumped back in disgust.

"It's a deer!" he gasped. "It's dead!"

"Only its body," said the hare, slowly sauntering towards Pridge and the deer before flopping back down at his feet.

"What am I supposed to do with this?"

"You needed a bone...."

"A sun-bleached bone! These bones have yet to even see the sun!"

"Well, that's not true," the hare yawned. "This animal has long since been scavenged by the other denizens of this wood. Many of its bones are quite bare."

Pridge looked down at the deer again. His lips curled up and nostrils flared as he looked over the carcass with discomfort. His pewter eyes scanned the body to see that the hare was right. There were many bones scattered about at his feet. He slowly knelt towards them and found the one he thought looked the cleanest. But the cleanest was a long shot from actually being clean. It was covered in dirt, yellow and reddish-brown stains, and flaked with a substance that Pridge didn't want to think about. He reached down, and while trying to touch it with as little of his hand as possible, held the bone between the tips of his forefinger and thumb.

"All right. One bone. What do I have to do next?"

"It isn't white as salt."

"You expect me to sun-bleach this bone? That will take ages!"

"That it will."

Pridge scoffed at the hare, but then he thought for a moment. "Well...if I paint the bone white as salt, will that count?"

"If you think so."

"Really?" Pridge puffed out his chest, happy to see his familiar so confident in him.

"Yes. But if you have any other ideas, I'm all ears."

Pridge could swear he saw the hare smirk. "Very funny." He picked up the hare and made his way out of the woods.

A while later, with one pristinely painted white bone at his side, Pridge was ready for his next task. Once again in Pridge's arms, the hare directed the boy to the hedges on the outskirts of the town. It hopped down and sat beside a set of large, stalked plants growing from the hedge.

"Milkweed lace," sighed the hare.

"What?"

"The next item you'll need is lace made from milkweed."

Pridge looked back and forward from the hare to the stalks. Then an exasperated frown sunk across his face. "You've got to be joking." The hare simply stared at him, unwavering in his instruction. "I don't know how to make lace! Much less from *milkweed*."

"Have you tried?"

"No! It's an incredibly difficult skill. I can't just do it."

"Maybe you should learn."

Pridge clenched his jaw in frustration for a good moment, but eventually, an idea struck him. He sat down beside the hare and smiled. "Very well. Could you show me? And once you're done, I can just do what you did."

The hare shrugged and turned towards the stalks. One by one, it pulled them down. In a surprisingly nimble fashion, especially for an animal without thumbs, Pridge watched as the hare stripped down the milkweed to thin fibers, quickly spun them into string, and began weaving the string into beautifully intricate lace. Although the hare made it seem easy with its bored expression and quick work, lacemaking looked to be a very difficult process.

Not before long, however, a large swatch of lace sat at Pridge's feet. "Incredible!" he said, picking it up and admiring its design.

"Your turn," the hare said.

"Of course," Pridge smiled slyly. "Oh, but wait a minute. We have milkweed lace right here! The spell doesn't call for two swatches, does it?"

"It does not," the hare replied.

"Well, we can just use this, can't we?"

"If you think so." The hare shrugged.

Pridge smiled and picked the hare up into his arms. He left the hedge, glad not to give it a second look. He now had a white bone and milkweed lace. The day wasn't even half over, and he'd already achieved two of the three tasks. Bristling with confidence, he was ready to retrieve the final item.

This time, the hare had Pridge take a bottle from home before heading to a river just past the edge of the forest. The water churned peacefully and provided a nice, cool place for Pridge to dip his feet into as he awaited further instruction.

"What was that final item?" he asked with a confident tone in his voice.

"The water which drowns a fallen star."

Pridge lifted his eyebrows in surprise and looked at the water at his feet. "Oh, my. This river drowned a star?"

"No," the hare responded in a sigh. "The river leads to a waterfall deep in the woods. At the top of those falls is where the star is drowned."

"A waterfall? You mean Devil's Edge Falls?"

"I believe that's what the townsfolk call it."

"They say the rocks are as sharp as blades and the water as hard as an avalanche. You expect me to climb that monstrosity for a *bottle of water?*"

"I expect you to do no such thing," the hare said, stretching himself across the grass for yet another nap.

Pridge stroked his chin as he looked down at the smooth water glistening in the forest light. He considered for a moment making the voyage to the horror at the other end of it. But then his eyes lit up bright as steel as he had another one of his brilliant ideas.

"If the falls are at the river's head, then they share the same waters, right?"

The hare shrugged in its half-asleep state, mumbling a sound of supposed agreement.

"Then if I take these waters, it's the same as going to the falls themselves, isn't it?"

"If you think so," the hare yawned.

Pridge let out an excited chuckle as he uncorked the vial and dunked it into the peaceful bath at his feet. Corking it again, he held it up, admiring the liquid swirling in the glass. Now, with all three ingredients cleverly collected, he was ready to brew his potion.

Eagerly, he prepared his household stregareum for the rite. Candles lit the room as the day came to an end. Every shelf, table, and lantern held a dripping taper. Spiders—who, as every witch knows, are a lucky sign in the stregareum—clung intently to their webs as they watched the boy work. A cast-iron cauldron was hung over a small firepit built into the center of the room.

Quite exasperated at the effort he had put into merely preparing the room, Pridge was ready to begin. A wooden table beside the cauldron had been adorned neatly with the "sun-bleached" bone, the lace he had "made" from milk-weed, and the water that "drowned a star."

"What do I need to do first?" Pridge asked, turning to the hare with a smug grin.

The hare sat at the foot of the table, slumped against the leg tiredly like a man who had eaten too much for dinner. It pawed at its face, cleaning its whiskers as it instructed in a bored voice, "spread the lace across the lip of the cauldron."

And Pridge did, stretching it to fit like a lid. He looked back to the hare for the next step.

"Pour the water through the lace to filter."

And Pridge did, watching sediment from the river catch into the fibers. He looked again to his familiar.

"Remove the lace and stir with the bone."

And Pridge did, spiraling the water like a vortex. Once more, he looked to the hare.

"That's it."

Pridge stared, confused for a moment, before looking disappointed again at the liquid. "That's it?"

"Mm-hmm."

"Do I drink it?"

"If you want."

Pridge, feeling as though he was missing something, skeptically reached for a ladle on the table. He dipped it into the lackluster waters and took a cautious sip. He smacked his lips, waiting for his great powers to surge into existence. The water was lukewarm, tasted a little like dirt, and cured him of some minor thirst. What it didn't do was grant him immeasurable magical abilities. He twisted his face in annoyance and shot the hare a look.

"I don't feel anything!"

"Were you expecting to?"

"That's what the potion is for isn't it? To awaken my hidden potential?"

"It is."

"But it isn't doing anything! I did everything right, didn't I?"

"If you think so."

"I do! I spent all day on this." He huffed and looked back at the cauldron. Maybe the potion simply just takes a while to work. That made sense. Why wouldn't it take a while? After all, with potential as great as his, it would be mad to assume such a thing could awaken instantly. Pridge was sure this was the case. So, with a confident nod, he put out the fire and all of the candles, took the hare into his arms, and headed to bed. Perhaps his potential would awaken within him in the morning.

That night, familiar images spun through his dreams. He saw a bone turning white in the sun; lace, laboriously made from milkweed; and water gathered from a deadly climb. These scenes flashed through his mind until morning came, and he jolted upright in his bed. As they faded from his thoughts, he recalled his excitement from the night before.

He took in a deep breath, and a smile spread across his face. The young witch dug deep to feel his newly awakened powers. But...he felt nothing. Nothing other than a lazy lump of fur cuddled up beside him. His eyebrows arched angrily, looking more like his father's than ever, and he shook the hare awake.

"Wake up! You messed something up! The potion didn't work at all!"

The hare, barely waking from slumber, mumbled back monotonously, "if you did everything right, then the potion worked."

"Well then it wasn't done right! You must have forgotten a step."

The hare turned over, its back to the young witch, drifting back to sleep even as it muttered, "no...I told you everything you need to know...."

Pridge was fuming. His blood boiled beneath his skin. This lazy familiar was utterly useless! Not only did it not seem to have a clue what it was doing, but it didn't even care in the slightest whether Pridge would succeed or not. The Oaken Wight must have succumbed to wood rot if it'd appointed this hare as a powerful spirit.

Well, if the hare couldn't be bothered to properly guide Pridge through its own potion, then he would just have to take the matter into his own hands. He got dressed, neatly flattened down his scruffy hair, and left the sleeping hare without even giving it a second look.

His first stop was to find his way back to the glade in the woods. After an exhausting effort attempting to find the same place, he finally recognized the sunny patch of grass between the trees. Scouring the shady corners of the glade, he once again found the carcass of the deer. Unfortunately, the bones hadn't seemed to have cleaned themselves up at all in the one day since he'd last seen them. Just as distasteful as he remembered.

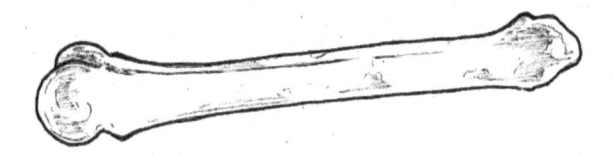

With his new stubbornness fueling him, however, he stomached up the courage to bend down and pick up a second bone. This one wasn't quite as clean as the first but was at least longer. He would need it to stir the potion, so that length would come in handy.

He got ready to leave the woods with it and fetch his white paint, until he recalled his dream of the bone whitening in the sun. *That will take forever,* he thought to himself. Although, it had been the hare that told him it was all right to paint the bone in the first place. And it did seem that the hare had more cotton in its head than on its tail. If he truly wanted to awaken his great potential, it would be best *not* to follow the hare's advice.

And so, he looked over the sunny glade and found the warm stone that the hare had laid across the day before. He placed the bone upon it and waited. After a few minutes, it was clear that the bone was not going to whiten before his very eyes. With a tired sigh, Pridge left the bone and made his way out of the woods. Perhaps tomorrow the bone would be white.

Next, he needed milkweed lace. This was going to be tricky. Pridge's mind pondered the possibilities as he trudged past the trees. He doubted he would be able to get the hare to make a second swatch. Nor did he want it to. Clearly, its handiwork was not up to snuff. But where would he even find more lace made of such a rustic material?

As he reached the edge of the forest, he crossed past the hedge of milkweed stalks that the two had sat by the day before. He stopped and glimpsed over his shoulder at the stalks. Pridge couldn't make the lace himself. He'd never done such a thing before. Although, he had watched the hare do it step by step the day before. And Pridge did think himself clever enough to remember the steps. *It can't be all that hard,* he thought.

This was incorrect. While the hare glided through the steps with ease, Pridge struggled to even strip the weed into threads. Each time he tried, the plant would bleed a white liquid onto his hands, making them sticky and hard to work with. It'd been well before noon when he'd started this project, and by the time he was just getting the hang of it, the sun was already setting.

He hated this. He hated every step of this. And yet, as he stripped his final stalk before heading home for the night, he felt a small surge of pride for how easily he seemed to master this part of the skill at least.

The next morning, Pridge rushed to the glade to check on the bone. It hadn't seemed to have changed at all. It truly was going to take forever to whiten. As he trudged out of the forest, he grumbled to himself how he was going to be an old man before he would see this task done. He crossed again over the hedge and mindlessly sat by the milkweed stalks as he stewed over his frustrations. His hands idly worked, stripping one stalk after another, and as hours went by and the sun began to set, he noticed that there were very few stalks left in the hedge. Looking down at the ground, Pridge saw that he had created more than enough milkweed thread to make his lace.

The next morning, he went again to check the bone, a basket of milkweed threads in hand. The bone remained unchanged. Disappointed, Pridge sat in the warm glade and began spinning the threads into yarn as the hare had shown him how to do. Making the thread alone had been hard, but this proved just as difficult. Still, as with the threads, he fell in rhythm with the process by the end of the day and started to spin some very handsome yarn.

This pattern repeated itself for days and weeks; he would check on the bone and spin his yarn in the glade. Eventually, he began the most difficult task of weaving the lace. The bone whitened day by day as he toiled, and once his lace was finally finished, the bone had become white as salt. He picked it up and admired the two items in his hand. No other bone was quite as pure, and no other lace was quite as beautiful. Of this, he was certain.

Although there was nothing easy about the first two tasks, they paled in comparison to the final one. But bolstered by these successes, Pridge was determined to take it on. This didn't mean he was by any means excited to do it. No, in fact, he was terrified. Once he found the river, every step forward filled him with even more regret.

By the time the dense forest began to block out the sun, Pridge felt as though his sweat was forming a river of its own. The woods themselves seemed to become less and less friendly as well. The soft, grassy soil gave way to uneven stones and dried earth; trees twisted higher and more menacingly; and the wildlife itself seemed to transform from sweet woodland creatures to bloodsucking pests and prowling shadows.

Finally, he reached Devil's Edge. The falls were twice as frightening as he had heard—and three times as ugly. It was hard to believe that something like this even existed in the forest and not only in his nightmares... though, he was sure it was going to make an appearance there too. *If* he was going to be lucky enough to have the chance to dream any nightmares after this.

Nevertheless, the witch boy took a deep breath, tightened the pack strapped high to his shoulders, and made his way towards the falls. He was ready for this. He'd made *milkweed lace*, after all. He could do anything.

As he got closer, heavy loads of water crashed beside him like stones. He was sure that if he got too close, he would be crushed to pieces. With a hard gulp, he reached out to a sharp rock jutting out from the wall of the falls and pulled himself up. After a few tiers of this, he realized it wasn't as hard as it looked. The rocks were actually rather easy to climb.

The comfort did not last, as "rocks as sharp as blades" was not an exaggeration. He cut his hands, arms, and knees making his way up the cliff. But he was almost at the top. Only a few more rocks and the star water was his!

Just as he got his grip on the last rock, his hand slipped on its wet surface. With his heart in his throat and his mouth in the toilet, he fell backwards. This was the end. He was going to die with nothing to his name but a bone, some lace, and a hare that could sleep through an earthquake. But suddenly, something like two small feet pushed hard against his back. This jolted him forward until he was against the wall once more. Frantically, he steadied himself, then turned to look behind him.

Just for a flash, he saw something like two long ears disappearing quickly into the mist. He was sure it was just his imagination. Now wasn't the time for that. With more bravery than he was worth, he reached again for the top of the cliff, and this time, pulled himself over the wall to safety.

There, at the top, everything seemed like another world. Instead of the tumult of cascading water and angry rocks, he found a plateau of grass and flowers surrounding the edges of a gentle spring. A light blue glow seemed to emanate from it, filling the misty air with etheric light. In the center of the spring sat a shimmering stone.

He knew exactly what it was, and without too much hesitation, he pulled the bottle from his pack and plunged it into the water. It filled with the luminous liquid, and Pridge filled with pride and joy along with it. This feeling stayed with him throughout the treacherous climb down the cliff, the trek through the forest, and the journey back home.

At last, he was ready to brew the potion again—the right way. He rushed to the stregareum, exhausted but full of energy. The hare came following in after him, hopping slowly like it had all the time in the world. Pridge was on no such clock. The candles were already lit and the fire bustling by the time the hare finally arrived in the room. Shadows danced into and out of corners as Pridge set the three items on the wooden table.

"You took your time acquiring these items," the hare said in its humdrum tone.

"Well, *your* way clearly wasn't working," Pridge replied, fastening the lace to the lip of the cauldron.

"It would seem not."

Pridge took the bottle of water in his hand. The faint blue glow stood out like lightning against the hard orange light of the fire. With bated breath, he uncorked the bottle and slowly poured the liquid over the lace. Passing through the fibers, it sizzled as it hit the hot iron of the cauldron. Now, removing the lace, he took up the bone. Pridge's heart was beating like thunder in his chest.

He placed the bone in the water and began to stir. First, he felt nothing, but then, everything. It struck him like a burst of water from the Devil's Edge, rushing into every fiber of his being. He finally realized what he was capable of. He could decipher the language of the stars, weave the fabric of fate itself, face the most insurmountable of odds!

"It worked!" Pridge gasped.

The hare smiled. "If you think so."

Pridge's face was bright with new energy. He was capable of so much now! There was no time to waste. He needed to get started. The witch boy grabbed books off of the shelves and vials from the cabinets. There was so much to learn. He couldn't wait for the next gathering when he could make his way down the old, crooked path again.

Bending Wood

Witch hazel, the bending wood,
Has more in common than it should
With the witch whose name it shares
And the qualities we bare.
There is much power in a word,
So dare we not speak lies, absurd
Lest our wills be then diluted
And spells we speak sit untransmuted.
But yet we bathe in mystery,
Of charms and paths and history.
To keep our secrets safe and whole,
Without a cause to pay the toll,
A witch's hallmark won't forsake
The truth of which we dare not break.
We will not lie, but are quite good
At bending truth like bending wood.

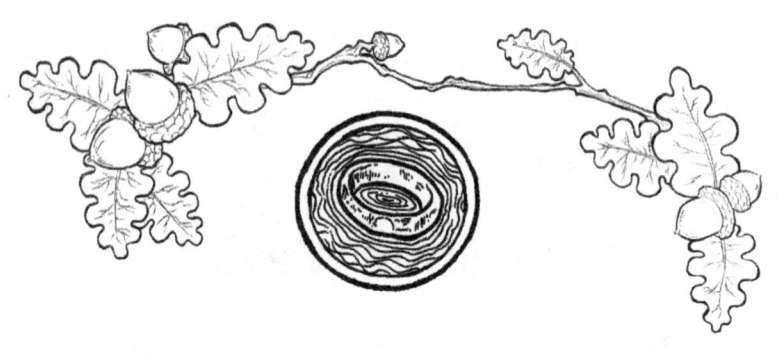

Chapter Five
The Vanishing Hovel

" ' **B**eware, little children, beware, beware, for these are the woods of the Seven Hides Witch!'" the storyteller read with a crackling voice to frighten the cluster of children gathered around her. They sat, leaning in with eyes as wide as blueberry pies, hanging on to every word. The storyteller continued: "'You'll know her by her low-hanging ears and a long tongue stained black with venomous tar! The earth itself turns to salt in her footsteps. She commands the wild beasts of the forests, and of the seven most vicious, she can take their likeness to seek out children just like you.'"

"Wh-what would sh-she do if she found us?" a pudgy blond-haired boy asked behind huddled knees.

"Ah. She'll use you to warm her wicked hearth, of course! But I'm sure none of you have anything to worry about, for it is the bones of naughty children that burn the brightest."

A mischievous smile hung on the storyteller's face as the children scattered away, back to their families. All of them, that is, except for young Adelaide Black. She lingered on every word of the tale as if trying to savor its exquisite flavor. Adelaide yearned more than anything to be just like the Seven Hides Witch. This was, of course, because unlike the other children in her village, Adelaide herself was a witch. She had no greater inspiration than the shape-shifting legendary sorceress herself.

Well, time passed from the days of dreamy childhood, and it was then that Adelaide found her chance to turn dreams into reality. She was twenty-four at the time, taller than most, with dark features, full lips, and a well-practiced sneer that could peel the skin off a turnip. These were only some of the unique traits she took with her to the borough of Cloughley.

Although it had not known a witch in all its years, the town was not without its superstitions. Every home had its horseshoe, and every person had their ghost story. Adelaide could not think of a better place to set up shop.

She was a sight as she strode into town, with her dark hair done up, her bejeweled neck dotted down, a cauldron in hand, and vials of potions strapped to her belt. There were very few locals who didn't turn their heads to look at her.

"Are you lost, miss?" an old, woolly man asked suspiciously as she sauntered past.

She merely turned her head to him, and with a graceless giggle, said, "not at all. I am Aunty Black, Cloughley's new witch."

With that, she left the woolly man benighted and bewildered—and maybe even a little bewitched. It wasn't long afterward that she became known throughout the borough. Rumor led to gossip, which led to report, which eventually led to clientele for the giddy woman.

People came from all around for a spell from Aunty Black.

"I'm haunted," one person proclaimed. "Will you exorcise it?" And she did.

"I'm poor," urged another. "Find me some money?" And she did.

"I'm sick," pleaded some. "Give me health?" And she did.

There were many requests, but none as sought after as love. Was it any surprise? It was the one thing that was insatiable in both its desire to gain and its desire to give.

It was this that brought the Princess of Cloughley's surrounding kingdom to Adelaide's door.

She was a woman, strict in appearance, aged somewhere in her late forties with tightly pinched hair and sharp, gaunt cheeks. "You are the self-proclaimed 'witch,' I presume?" the princess said, carefully lowering herself onto the couch in Adelaide's parlor. Two heavily armored guards stood against the walls of the cozy room.

"You're not a believer?" Adelaide asked in her sly, gruff voice as she set a tray of tea in front of the princess.

"I believe in results." The princess took up a cup and held it in her bony fingers. "Can you give me results?"

"I can," Adelaide said confidently, easing herself into a chair across from the couch. "What kinds of results do you wish for?"

The princess took a sip of the tea, shooting an uncomfortable glance at her guards from behind the cup. Placing it back down, she composed her expression and waved the guards out of the room. After a moment of hesitation, they marched outside the witch's cottage and stood guard on the front steps.

"There is a man," the princess began.

"Isn't there always," Adelaide said with a friendly snort.

"I would thank you not to interrupt me," the princess replied coldly. Adelaide's

smile dropped as she sat to nervous attention. The princess continued. "He is a noble man, handsome and dependable. However, his wife stands in my way. I need him to leave her. Then he can love only me." The princess stared at Adelaide, taking another sip of her tea.

"You... want me to separate their marriage?"

"Is that a problem? Or are you unable to perform the feats that you claim?"

Adelaide's dark eyes fixed upon the woman nervously, then towards the shadow of the armored men behind the window. She took a deep breath and said reluctantly, "I can do it."

And so, the two proceeded with the witch's spells. The next few days continued quietly. Adelaide brewed her potions and tended her herbs. She even had time to peruse through some of the books in her collection.

One day, dressed in her raggedy, old work aprons, Adelaide placed her large iron cauldron on a steady flame in the front garden of her little cottage. She was muddling a very delicate potion; one wrong measurement could cause quite the kerfuffle.

To her sudden confusion, a band of Cloughley's residents came rounding the corner to her cottage. They stopped at the small garden wall separating the witch's home from the street. Adelaide stood beside her cauldron, watching the crowd with nervous expectation.

The princess and her guards stepped their way through the crowd and stood before the witch. The princess, with a steely anger in her voice, spoke to her loud enough for the crowd to hear.

"Adelaide Black, as the princess over Cloughley, I am placing you under arrest for *fraud*."

"Wh-what?" Adelaide gasped. "Fraud?"

"I have testimony from several of your previous clients. Where you promised wealth, freedom, and...*love*, no evidence of such outcomes has been achieved."

"I don't understand—"

"I told you once, Miss Black, I don't like to be interrupted." The princess took a step towards the witch and spoke in a quiet tone. "And I certainly don't like being made a fool of. I hold a lot of pull over this town. You will be lucky if I don't have you executed for this."

Adelaide's dark face went pale. She stood before her neighbors in vulnerable disarray. For the first time, she saw the hint of a smile on the princess's face. And a cruel one at that. The cold woman motioned to her guards to take Adelaide away.

Dutifully, the guards approached the garden's gate. What was Adelaide to do? They stepped onto her grass, trampling her lavender in the process. She needed to think quickly. They reached for her. What could she do? But she just stood there, dumb with her bubbling cauldron and a vial of iron dust in hand—

"Oh!" she yelped, just as one of the guards took hold of her shoulder. The witch emptied the vial into the cauldron, and almost instantaneously, a large black cloud emerged, sparking and howling like a parade of lost souls.

Once the cloud finally dissipated, the witch was nowhere to be seen.

"*Find her!*" the princess bellowed.

Adelaide had quite the lead on everyone, though. She was halfway past the briars at this point, well into the woods. Her apron and sleeves had caught on the thorns as she struggled past them; her arms bled from scratches. Still, Adelaide made it to the boundary of the forest's shadow. Triumphantly, she stepped into its safety, away from Cloughley.

Although the sun had not yet set, the woods were very dark. Shadows became cavernous, trees were only blackened silhouettes, and even the sounds of the forest seemed to fall away into an echoing void.

The less she was able to see with her eyes, though, the more her witch's sight seemed to pick up. Shimmers of spirits passed through the trees like underwater shadows. They flitted past her tattered skirts and rustled her tangled hair. Mortals were one thing, but the dealings of spirits? *That* she was familiar with. A sense of peace overcame her, and the witch could finally take a breath of relief.

A Witch's Book of Terribles

In the distance, covered by darkness, a large figure watched her. It was hard to make out any details aside from the sheer size of it, but it did seem to lack the mirage-like features that most spirits exhibited. In her peaceful daze, she stared longer than she noticed.

Then, without warning, the figure burst from its place behind the trees and sped towards her. Her body reacted faster than her mind did as she turned tail and ran deeper into the woods. What was chasing her? One of the princess's guards? An angry spirit? A bear? Were the woods beginning to play tricks on her mind?

Branches broke behind Adelaide as the *thing* continued its pursuit. The darkness around her formed shapes; for a second, she swore she could even see an old hovel with a tall, pointed roof appear out of nowhere.

A warm light suddenly spread a soft glow as it flickered from the hovel's window. Was this not a trick? Did she

really see a house? Adelaide didn't have time to question herself. She stumbled clumsily to the door. Before she could even knock, the door eased open. She hesitated only a moment before quickly rushing inside and slamming the door closed behind her.

Adelaide leaned back against the door, struggling to catch her breath for many moments before taking the chance to survey her new surroundings. Wooden walls smelled of rustic cedar, little trinkets and decorative ornaments hung from the rafters, and a warm hearth was happily aglow. It took a bit for Adelaide to notice the old woman casually sitting in a cushioned chair beside the fire.

"Ahh!" Adelaide jumped. "Terribly sorry, ma'am. I— there was something outside, and...." Adelaide hurried to fix the black thicket of hair on her head into something presentable as she attempted to explain herself.

"Oh, don't trouble yourself with that, love," the old woman chuckled as she poured herself a glass of mead. "No sense in trying to impress around here. Heaven knows I'm not going to put in the effort."

Adelaide watched the old woman and let out one of her gruff giggles. She was beginning to feel at ease again. Looking the woman over, Adelaide noted the short peppery white hair brushing her endearingly large ears, the dark lips spread happily across rosy cheeks, and a face lined with years of smiles. Though she was small, the woman's presence seemed as if it filled the room to its very corners.

"Well, don't stand there all night, love." The woman smirked as she poured another glass of mead. "You're not going to make this old biddy drink alone, are you?"

Adelaide smiled and sat beside her in a chair with its back to the warm fire. She sipped on the sweet mead, which seemed to soothe every ache and scrape she had. "Thank you for letting me in," she said. "My name is Adelaide."

"Call me Lattie. It really has been too long since I've had another witch as company." The old woman put down her mead and began to chew on a stick of black licorice from her pocket.

"*Another* witch? You mean you're one too?"

"I suppose you know a lot of *non*-witches living alone in disappearing houses in the woods, do you?"

Adelaide snorted and shook her head. "Well, it seems bloody obvious when you say it that way." The two shared a smirk. Adelaide then glanced at the woman's lips, which were now stained black from the licorice.

"How rude of me. Would you like some?" Lattie reached for another stick of licorice, but it fell out of her pocket onto the floor. "Oops! These old hands haven't gotten any less clumsy it seems."

"Let me," Adelaide insisted, bending down to pick it up. As she did, she found a small dusting of white powder by the woman's feet. Salt? With a sudden rush of understanding, Adelaide filled with both fear and exhilaration. She jumped up to her feet as if being pulled by the collar and shouted, much to Lattie's surprise, "you're the Seven Hides Witch!"

The old woman just stared back at her in a state of shock. Then, her black mouth opened wide as she let out a hard belly laugh. "What gave me away? It was the big ears, wasn't it?"

"The salt...actually." Adelaide was beginning to shrink back into herself. Maybe she shouldn't have announced her realization so readily. "It's said that the earth turned to salt wherever she...you...stepped."

The Seven Hides Witch pulled herself up from her chair. She was hunched over and small but had the presence of a thunderstorm. She reached toward Adelaide, her dark, stained teeth glinting in the firelight. The young witch backed slowly away from her, closer and closer towards the burning hearth. Just as she reached the mantle, she tripped and fell towards the flames.

"Careful!" Lattie warned, even as Adelaide's chair sprung from its corner and caught her before falling into the fire.

Adelaide sat stiffly in the chair, waiting for her thoughts to catch up with her. "You're not going to kill me?"

"Kill you?" Lattie said, reaching for another log to throw on the fire. "I don't find myself in the business of killing house guests, my dear."

"But you're the Seven Hides Witch."

"Aye," she said as she cozied back into her seat.

"You're not really as...scary as the stories made you seem."

"Oh, I'm plenty scary," Lattie smiled, "when I have the mind to be. But some stories can skew over time." She reached down to her slipper and peeled it off. Salt poured out from the sole and onto the floor.

"You fill your shoes with salt?"

"To keep away the evil spirits. Can't be too careful."

Adelaide looked at Lattie's lips. "And your mouth isn't full of venomous tar...it's just licorice?"

"One of my vices," the old woman said, pulling out another piece from her pocket.

"It's all slander, then? Just stories told to make you look bad?"

"Stories are all about point of view, love," she said in a long sigh. "And a good story can be told to three different people with three different reactions. Truth is only what you make of it, of course."

Adelaide smiled and sunk back into the chair. She let out a wistful breath and gazed into the fire. "I doubt my own story will end with quite as much depth."

"How are you going to already determine how it ends when it has barely even begun?"

"You don't understand. I've been branded a fraud. If I go back to Cloughley, they'll have me executed."

"*Cloughley?*" The old witch made a face of disgust. "Dreadful little borough, that one. Passed through it once. Neediest crowd of prosy-folk I've ever seen."

Adelaide snorted. "Fair assessment, I must say. Still, if my spells didn't work, then they didn't work."

"Didn't they, though?"

"What do you mean?"

The Seven Hides Witch took a final swig of her mead and leaned in creakily towards Adelaide. "I'm going to teach you something that I have taught to few others."

She stood up and slowly made her way to the windowsill, where a small candle stood. She picked it up and brought it back to Adelaide. Upon closer inspection, she could see that instead of a holder, the taper had been nestled into the bones of a small animal, like that of a toad.

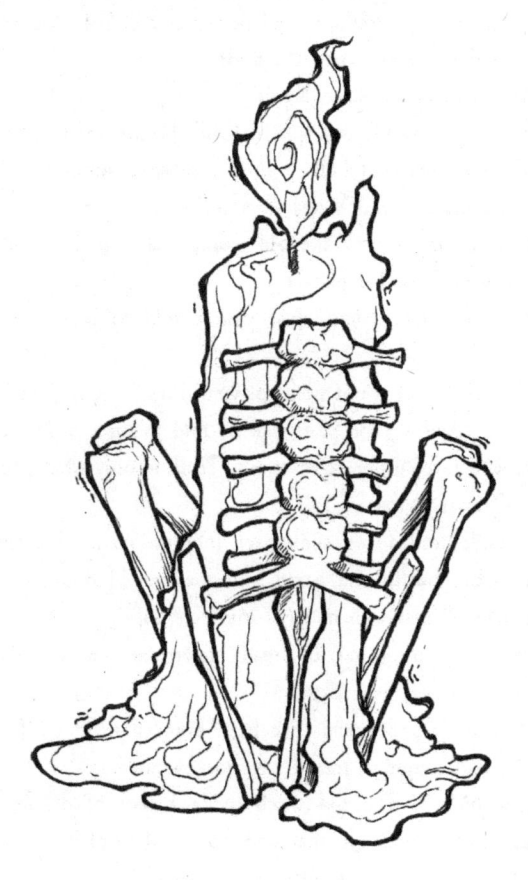

"This candle," Lattie began, "was formed under the round moon's light from the fats of those who walk, slither, swim, and fly. It is unique in its virtue as it is in its making."

"I'm not sure I understand."

Lattie held up her finger and pulled from it a rough amber ring, handing this to Adelaide as well. "Do not worry. It is in fact, quite simple. You will ignite the candle and gaze at its flame through the ring. Speak these words of truth upon it:

> *Time shall pass the moon and sun,*
> *Life and death are two in one.*
> *By the earth who yearns the sky,*
> *And the rain that fills its ply,*
> *With finick, fine, and further truth,*
> *Turn flesh and foot and tail and tooth.*

Speak this truth, and it shall reveal truth. Then, place the ring beneath your tongue and wait."

"Wait for what?"

"You'll know when it happens, love." The Seven Hides Witch smirked and stood herself up. With that, she hobbled away, up the stairs of the hovel, into the darkness.

Adelaide sat, confused as to what her next steps should be. But what else did she have to lose at this point? With a nod of determination, she lit the wick with the hearth's flame and steadied the candle in front of her. Peering at its flickering light through the ring, she spoke the words of truth. Then, as Lattie instructed, Adelaide placed the ring under her tongue and waited.

Suddenly, she felt something begin to change. Her blood turned hot, and her muscles wound up tight. The skin on her bones began to grow itchy. She felt as though it was going to fall right off her body. Just then, as if on cue, the candle's flame extinguished itself. As it did, Adelaide's skin split and fell off of her like a winter coat.

In fear she looked down at her arms, but instead of blood, she saw white fur covering lean paws. She examined further, finding herself to have a curled white tail, pricked ears, and a wet snout.

"Ah, a dog, is it?" Lattie said, descending the stairs. "Loyal and trusting, but fierce."

Adelaide opened her mouth to speak, but only a whimper came out.

"Not in this shape, love. You have taken the form of your true animal. Everyone has at least one. I suspect, over time, you may acquire even more."

Adelaide opened her maw to spit out the ring, but the old witch stopped her.

"Not yet. Not until your work is done. In this form, you can return to Cloughley. Find what you need to learn. Then, once your peace is made, return the ring to me and you shall regain your human skin." She opened the thick wooden door with a squeak and motioned the white dog towards the woods. "Go on, now. Trust the animal. It will show you the way."

Adelaide was understandably hesitant. She hadn't even taken the time to process what had just happened. But with a quick shooing from the old witch, she scampered out into the dark.

The animal will show me the way? What does that mean? As the thoughts passed through her mind, though, something else came in. A scent. Lavender, perhaps? It beguiled the dog, and she found herself trotting between trees through the darkness. The shadows began to lift, and soon enough, she found herself running out of the forest, over the briars, and back to her garden in Cloughley where her lavender remained trampled in the dirt.

It happened so quickly—the animal truly had shown the way. And it wasn't over yet. She heard a voice in the distance. Before her mind could act, her feet did, rushing her through the streets to the sound. She stopped at a small house where a distressed woman stood in her kitchen. Adelaide recognized her as someone who came to her once regarding a haunting. And from the looks of things, she was still in the midst of it.

"No! Not again!" The woman scowled as she opened her bread pantry to find it empty. "The food disappeared again! That lousy witch. She couldn't remove but one ghost!"

Adelaide felt her heart sink. But then, another sound—a scurrying coming from the walls. Looking down, just by her white paws, she saw a line of fat mice rushing from a small crevice in the wall, leaving behind a trail of breadcrumbs.

Mice? Adelaide thought. *It's they who have been stealing her food! No wonder my spell didn't work. She was never haunted to begin with.*

A moment later, another voice overtook her, and her feet sent her running. One scene after another, the witch saw more of the same. She was taken to the man who'd asked for wealth, and he had indeed been granted it, but wasting all of his treasure on decadence, he'd fallen again into poverty. Next, she was taken to the woman who'd asked for healing; the woman's unhealthy living habits had deprived her of any health Adelaide may have given her.

It was the last person she was taken to that she found the most interesting. She found herself watching a handsome man from outside a large manor. He sat in his drawing room, gazing solemnly at a golden wedding ring. This must have been the man that the princess pined for. The witch's spell had worked. His marriage had broken, and yet, this alone was not enough to drive him into the princess's arms as she expected.

This knowledge chuffed the witch-dog; it wasn't *her* bewitchments that failed the princess's plan. The feeling was quickly replaced, however, with regret. It was now for nothing that this man suffered. She bowed her head and turned from the manor.

As the day ran out, she trotted back to the briars at the forest's edge. She barely snagged herself this time on thorns as she skipped into the shadows. Like before, the woods darkened, and spirits crooned through the trees. Amidst the inky blackness, a pointed house with orange glowing windows appeared from thin air. Luckily, this time, she didn't need to be chased by one of Lattie's beasts to find it.

Adelaide stood her furry feet on the front steps and dropped the ring from under her tongue. The door creaked open as the ring rolled inside; the Seven Hides Witch stepped out, holding Adelaide's skin.

"Well, it seems you do prefer the comforts of your own skin after all," Lattie smiled, patting the dog's head. She draped the skin over Adelaide, saying:

> *"With finick, fine, and further truth,*
> *Turn flesh and foot and tail and tooth."*

The young witch quickly found herself kneeling on the ground, reformed in her womanly shape.

"Well?"

Adelaide patted the dried leaves off her skirt as she stood. "I have a lot of work to do."

"I'm glad to hear it." Lattie smiled. "Show them what a witch you are."

"Thank you, Lattie. For everything."

Lattie gave Adelaide a little wink and stepped back into her house. The door disappeared, and then the walls, and finally the glow of the windows. Adelaide was alone again, but she was empowered. And good thing, because as she'd said, she had a lot of work to do.

A small mob had formed in Cloughley's town square. All of the people that Adelaide had visited as a dog were there, but of course, they were rallied by the princess herself. She stood on a dais in her tightly sewn, pristine dress, announcing to the mob:

"I don't care where you have to look! Cloughley is not about to bend to the trickery of one so-called witch. Bring her back here, and I will ensure that Aunty Black, the *Addled Witch*, pays for her deceit!"

"Addled, am I?" Adelaide said calmly as she approached the mob.

All faces turned to look at her, the princess's most sharply. A creaky smile grew across her cheeks. "Come to face your punishment, have you?"

Adelaide stepped into the center of the crowd. They slowly backed away in the wake of her eerie calm, creating a ring around her. "You know, I learned recently that one story can have many outcomes."

"I'm afraid you only have one outcome, today—"

"Do not interrupt me, please," Adelaide said sternly. The princess was taken aback, twisting her face in offense. Adelaide continued, "now, I wonder how the outcome would change if more of the story was revealed."

She pulled out a little teacup from her satchel. It was the same cup that each client in the mob had at one point drunk from in Adelaide's little parlor. If they'd been willing to empty the cup's contents from its porcelain lip, perhaps Adelaide could use it to empty something from their lips.

"Speak this truth, and it shall reveal truth," she muttered to herself. The witch held the cup out before her, and the townsfolk took another step back as she incanted:

> *"You have paid, and I've paid twice,*
> *Let this third annul the price.*
> *Your lips have taken, and they'll give,*
> *The truth, the shame, my right to live!"*

She reached quickly into her satchel again and pulled out the earnings paid by the townsfolk. She dropped one coin into the cup; a wind moved through the crowd as the coin chimed against the base.

Just then, a voice peeped up from the silence: "I wasted all the wealth Adelaide conjured for me!" It was the poor man who'd asked the witch for money. He clasped his hands to his mouth in surprise.

Adelaide smiled slyly and dropped another coin into the cup. This was met with a confession from the unhealthy woman, which was followed by another coin and another confession, and so on and so on. The princess grew increasingly nervous at this. The handsome man had edged his way next to the princess as he watched the ruckus in awe. She turned her attention from the townsfolk to him and back again.

"Catch her! Catch that Addled Witch!" she yelped, flinging her arms in the air. But most of the townsfolk hadn't heard her amongst the chatter, and those who had simply didn't care anymore.

The princess looked over and locked eyes with Adelaide who stood still in the hectic crowd with a clenched fist held over the teacup. The princess shook her head pleadingly, but Adelaide was far past sympathy. She opened her fist, and one last coin dropped into the cup.

With that, the princess turned to the handsome man, and like wind bursting through an open door, said, "I caused your marriage to fail so that you would love me!" He looked at her in betrayed shock. But it didn't stop there.

She further confessed to turning everyone against Adelaide, to false convictions she'd made in her favor, to stealing from the treasury, and it went on. The whole mob grew silent as she listed her confessions. Even Adelaide was dumbfounded at the success of her spell.

Once the princess was done, she stood shocked and withered like a bag that had all of the air blown out of it. Silence filled the square. One after another, everyone turned to the witch expectantly.

"Why are you looking at me?" she snorted. "*You're* the angry mob." At this, she turned away, back to her cottage with teacup in hand. It would be untrue if she said she wasn't pleased to hear the sound of the princess screaming as she was rushed out of town by dozens of angry people.

Always Waiting

Take thyself to the all-lost hours,
  Where night things wander rife with power.
Where skins are shed,
And vows are bled,
And where we tend forgotten dead.
One witch came here as a child,
Her heart was full, her wishes wild.
Spirits told,
Beyond the fold,
Of all things more than silver and gold.
But prosy-folk, another kind,
Their world's seen magic left behind.
Not one ghost,
Among their host,
And never witches by their coast.
One peccadillo on her end,
The girl, she turned to prosy trends.
Thus, her wonder,
Changed to blunder,
As child's ways, they fell asunder.
Magic hides from those who jade,
And so, her witch's blood would fade.
But should she scour,
We won't sour,
Waiting at the all-lost hours.

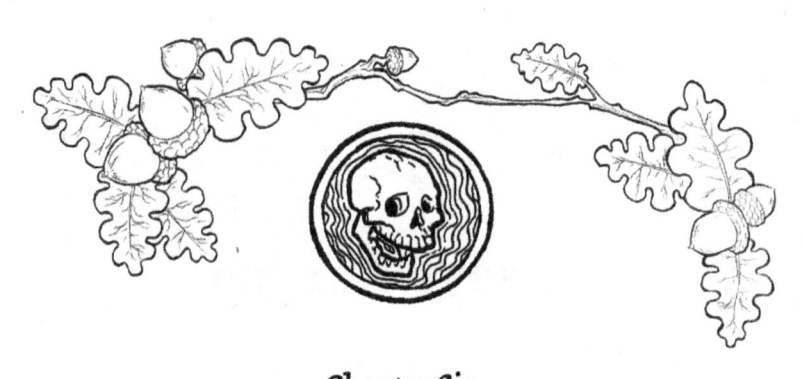

Chapter Six
Two Brothers and the Blood Wedding

The day of the big wedding finally arrived, and everyone seemed to have been invited. Grimlies popped out of their copper kettles, Knotwood Sprites shifted their spirits away from the trees, the Spider Barons were dressed in their finest silks, and even the Frost Wraiths momentarily ceased their plagues to join in the fun. In fact, it was rumored that Death herself was presiding over the rite. And why wouldn't she? This was a wonderful occasion. It was the union of the mysterious Waylon Blood and Periwinkle Pennyknuckle, our beloved Stone Maid.

Blood was who they had to thank for the weather in these parts—and for safety in travel along all roads, from the heaths to the bluffs. And the Stone Maid was responsible for the growth of wildflowers as she ate her stone fruits and discarded their pits. These, of course, were blooming into a variety of beautiful flora now decorating the roads that Waylon Blood would guard.

It was this union that all manner of being not only appreciated for its rustic beauty, but also relied upon to predict how the winds might turn across Blood's roads. When the maid's flowers were open wide, it was a sign that she had recently walked those roads, and so Blood would ensure good weather for her. If the petals had closed to sleep, however, it was a sign that she had not walked those roads in quite some time, and so a storm was likely to brew.

Even the sour Mallory Munchett, who held disdain for all except her lemons, respected the marriage and attended the ceremony. Even if her face did seem even more pursed than usual at the idea of it.

Now, all of this being said, there did happen to be two brothers among the local congregation who were not invited. One, Casper, tall with a young beard that masked his codgerly disposition; the other, Pendleton, stocky with deep-set eyes as cold as an autumn wind. These brothers weren't known for their congeniality nor their goodwill. What they were known for was their insatiable taste for mischief and unquenchable penchant for power. Because of this, it seemed as though every measure had been taken to hide the day of the wedding from the brothers—presumably so as not to disrupt the already fragile tensions of the attendees.

This attempt was, of course, a failure. As our story would have it, the two brothers were a pair of witches—and rather devious ones at that. Once the event was revealed to them in their divinations, they determined it to be a perfect opportunity to make their mark among such a rare gathering of legendary figures. After all, what figure could be more legendary than that of Death?

The great doors to the temple opened, and the company filled its ancient hall. These walls were old, and no one knew anymore who'd built them, but it was clear that they no longer belonged to man. It was a place that felt stoic and noble. However, high in the rafters, the tone had grown bitter where two interlopers had dedicated themselves to their nefarious deeds.

Casper and Pendleton smiled at each other with devilish excitement as they straddled the wooden beams. Below them, a mismatched potluck of mythical figures took their seats. The air itself was thick with magic in the presence of such a menagerie.

As time passed and neither the bride, groom, nor presider made their entrance, the brothers became antsy. This got the best of Pendleton once he spotted Mallory Munchett in the crowd. She was easily recognizable, sitting stiffly with her high Elizabethan collar and a lemon tight in her hand, which she contently sucked on.

"Watch this," he said, nudging Casper. The witch pulled out a small twig, bound with magic by waxen herbs. Holding it in two hands, he muttered to himself:

> *"Prickledy flick, thick in the trick,*
> *Stricken and quicken, snicketty stick!"*

With that, he split the item in two.

Almost instantly, Mallory Munchett jumped up from her seat as if a ball of nettles had fallen down her dress. The lemon flew from her hand and landed hard between the pews in front of her. Where

every drop of juice spilled, a thicket of thistles sprouted and hairy celandines spread across the aisle.

The brothers choked back laughter at the sight of it all. Casper, then seeing Mad-Mouthed Routh attempt to avoid sitting on a bushel of Mallory's thistles, took some coins from his pocket and poured them into a small pouch. He drew a circle with chalk onto the rafter and dropped the pouch into its center. With this, Mad-Mouthed's left side seemed to double in weight, causing him to tilt over onto the thistles. And, true to his name, he began to regurgitate words so foul that it drove all those around him into a mad frenzy.

Nearly falling from the ceiling, the witch brothers wheezed and gasped for air between what reprieve their laughter would give them. Casper then noticed Madame Pepperdy—the old phantom who haunted the Bone River Pass—was craning her unusually long neck over the crowd to see the commotion. He pulled a braided cord from his pocket, anointed it with three drops of a foul-smelling oil, looked at her through a loop in the cord, and uttered a short charm:

"Rivers run, but the North sends frost; yet you're the one to pay the cost. Now rivers run, but you may not!"

Casper then jerked the cord into a quick knot.

Suddenly, Madame Pepperdy's knees buckled, causing her to fall into a ghostly heap between Luffanee Rye, the funeral fiddler, and an equine imp. Amidst flustered apologies and the witches' giggles as Pepperdy attempted to untie herself, Pendleton took the cord and tied the knot into a bigger knot, then another knot over that. This stuck the imp, the phantom, and the fiddler together as if they were glued, causing them to struggle and fall across their whole row.

The brothers began to feel lightheaded with magical fatigue, but nonetheless, they let their competition get the best of them. Pendleton lit a small candle made of beeswax and scarecrow hay. With this, he began to cast shadow puppets onto the rafters, which slithered away from him into the crowd, resulting in many startled jumps and yelps. Casper gathered a handful of dust, and with the utterance of a quick incantation, swallowed it. Below him, many began to sneeze and cough.

The entire assembly had become utter pandemonium, and the two witches were relentless. Whether they were competing with each other or themselves, at this point, their spells had brought them to exhaustion. With blurred vision and an almost starved state of euphoria, the two grew desperate for an excuse to save what little bit of magic still remained within them.

At that, the doors to the temple suddenly creaked open, slowly, like a drawbridge. As they did, a hush fell over the crowd. Waylon Blood and Periwinkle Pennyknuckle stepped past the threshold, arm in arm. Whether they noticed it or not, their faces made no reaction to the tumult in the temple. The two simply stepped forward down the aisle, and as they did, the attendees all rushed quietly back to their seats, parting before the betrothed like a curtain.

Even the brothers had become docile, their eyes transfixed on Blood and the Maid. The figures looked like they had just stepped out of the pages of a fable. Blood walked like the calm before a storm, clad with skins and antlers from carrion of the roads. The Stone Maid, on the other hand, exuded that which likened to the refreshing shade of a hot day, supplied with her familiar wooden shoes and a wicker basket.

Just then, a musk of perfumed flowers and deep earth filled the hall. The brothers brushed away the exhaustion from their pallid faces as their excitement once again grew.

"It's Death!" Casper said in a whispered gasp.

"Finally!" Pendleton quietly cheered as a shadow slowly approached the doorway.

The witches readied themselves now for their final spell. They reached deep into their veins to pull what power their blood still held—but soon found that not even a glimmer remained. They looked at each other in exasperation.

Everyone in the temple below was now silent as the grave, unmoving and unblinking, waiting for Death to appear. The wood of the temple was creaking under the weight of her infamy alone. This anticipation was deadly.

Sweat dripped from strands of Casper's and Pendleton's brassy hair. They were now mining their very marrow for any shred of magic that they might still possess. Years seemed to fall from them like leaves as they rattled and groaned for air.

The spirit of a single rosebud heard their struggle amongst the temple's bated breath. She looked up to the rafters first, then was followed by Peppermint Tom and Milk Mary May. One after another, the congregation lifted their heads to the rafters.

It was of course Mad-Mouthed Routh who broke the stillness, his voice bellowing through the silence like a bitter, cold wind. "*Witches!*"

A heartbeat passed before either of the brothers registered what they had heard. With one final breath, Casper and Pendleton looked shakily under the rafters. Their veins turned to ice as they noticed every single face in the temple below them glaring back to meet their eyes. Each face grew angrier than the next as the congregation pieced together the chaotic events of the day.

This took the last that the brothers had. With darkening vision and numbed balance, they fell from the rafters like dead flies into the ravenous pit of the assembly.

It was then that Death finally arrived.

The Stars in Her Hair

There once was a girl as young as a bud,
With long curly hair, the color of blood.
A bonny belle, so fond of her looks,
She shunned of her talents, the mill, and her books.
But oh, how she yearned for the moon and the stars,
How do they feel near when they shimmer so far?
This she was sure, there's a star of her own,
For when it may sparkle, she tastes honeycomb.
She'll smell then raspberry and feel feather down,
And nary she's left wearing a frown.
It spins for her dreams that sweeten her nights,
And tells her of ways that lead her through plights.
Little by little the girl cared for more,
Than ribbons and rouges and rubies she wore.
This ivory light, it taught her of things,
To mend and to make and what words to sing.
And as a reward, a mark she could bear,
The starlight would fasten itself to her hair.
With every new virtue the girl came to find,
Another bright strand would fasten in kind.
And should come the day, she's
grown to their par,
Will her ivory light
be another bud's star.

Chapter Seven
Neverfair

Poor Hortense. Not only was she not pretty, but she was painstakingly plain. In fact, the girl seemed to possess the uncanny ability to blend into the scenery with all the skill of a roll of wallpaper. She only wanted to be noticed, but with her lackluster hair, sallow skin, and unflattering shape, she'd be lucky to be noticed as a bump on the road, much less a girl. Yes, young Hortense was uniquely uninspiring.

At home, things weren't much better. Her parents, both sharing none of her features (or lack thereof), couldn't understand her plight if they tried. Her mother was tall with the silkiest curls framing her pretty face. Her father's dimpled chin was only outmatched by the broadness of his shoulders.

"You have nothing to worry about!" her father assured her with his deep brown eyes. "It's the beauty of the heart that matters."

"You'll grow into your looks," her mother said behind a ruby-lipped smile. "Once you find yourself, everything else will fall into place!"

However, these words might as well have been a raindrop on an inferno for all the help they were. All the sweet comforts in the world couldn't make Hortense beautiful, could they? They weren't magic spells, after all.

Well, Hortense went on, drifting along from day to day as invisible as the wind. At school, she was never called on in class, never picked for teams, never looked at by the boys she loved. And, of course, she loved them all. She had so much to give if only someone would let her have the chance.

When her woes overtook her, she often went to find a quiet place to relax and mull in her unrequited loves. The town she lived in was very old and tended to have many abandoned buildings just on the outskirts of the population. One such place she liked to visit was a rickety old mill that surely hadn't seen another person for decades. This of course invited many rumors. "An old witch once lived there!" "The land is cursed!" "No one in their right mind would visit that spooky mill." These rumors never repelled Hortense, however. After all, one of the benefits of being so lonely was that no matter where you went, you were always surrounded by all your friends.

The only other living creatures that even frequented the mill were packs of slithering snakes. This, more than any other reason, was probably why the mill had been abandoned for so long. Ophidiophobia—a fear of snakes. She didn't mind them, though, and they didn't mind her either. At times, it seemed as if the snakes even enjoyed her company. Whenever that thought entered the young girl's head, though, she would quickly stamp it out. Her life was sad enough. She wasn't about to start confusing apathy with friendship.

After school one particularly unpleasant day, she wandered to the old mill. So lost in longing, she fell into an almost dream-like state as she listened to the rhythmic hissing of the snakes that followed her steps through the mill.

"I wish people would be as welcoming to me as you are," Hortense sighed to the snakes. She trudged along, moping and pulling out tall grasses to play with between her fingers—until suddenly, she heard a voice.

"*Ssso* be it."

The girl gasped and looked around. "Who's there?" Was it her imagination? Wind rustling through the leaves?

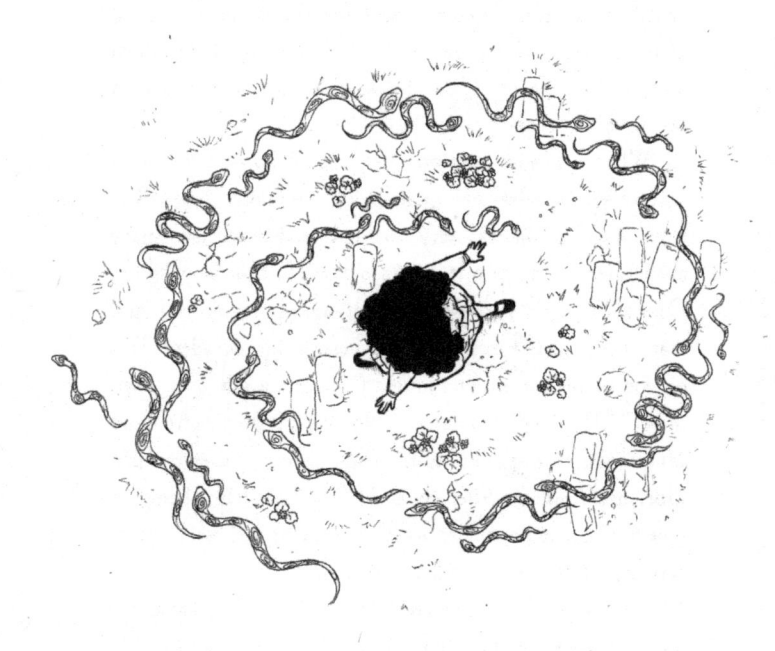

"We can make them *sssee* what we *sssee*."

She looked down to find the snakes looking her in the eyes, waiting patiently for her reply. "Was...was that you? Can you speak?" A moment of silence passed. Enough for

Hortense to feel silly for thinking that snakes could talk. But then one opened its mouth, and a single word fell out like steam from a pot.

"*Yesss.*"

She let out a yelp and jumped backward. Her foot caught on a crumbled old wooden step, and she fell flat on her back. Her beige ruffled skirt was tangled up in a bush, and her unruly, dull hair jutted out at odd angles. She portrayed a truly unflattering image.

The snakes slithered up to her, slowly hissing, "you are not *ssso* hopelesss, Hortenssse."

Well, this was hard to believe, coming from reptiles or not. Hortense let out a light scoff as she struggled to untangle her skirt from the bush.

"Lisssten, and we can help you appear beautiful."

Sitting up straight and attempting to flatten her hair, Hortense dared to give the snakes a glance of interested curiosity. They were already talking snakes, after all. What could another mote of belief hurt at this point?

The snakes, sensing her acceptance, coiled into a circle around her. Hissing in an almost choir-like unison, they spoke:

> *"To get you must give of what you would gain,*
> *Place this within a bowl 'fore thee lain.*
> *Fill it with milk of pure alabassster,*
> *Sssoak in the ssskin from the one we call massster.*
> *Ssstir this about with the hoof of a mare,*
> *Until the ssscales are plump and fair.*
> *Take to your lipsss and ssswallow it whole,*
> *Then find in the morning, your beauty extolsss."*

Hortense was understandably puzzled. Something about the skin of a master and a hoof? Was it some kind of a riddle? A lesson that would make sense in time? Well, no. She would find everything the snakes told her to be quite literal.

A Witch's Book of Terribles

When returning home that night, Hortense placed a bowl upon her vanity table. She put into it that which she would gain—this being a strand of her hair which she wished more beautiful, as well as a ribbon tied around her waist which she wished thinner. She then filled the bowl with milk of pure alabaster, untainted and freshly bought from the market.

"The skin of the master" she figured would be more trouble to attain, but the snakes solved that problem for her. After their rhyme, the largest snake in the pit slithered up to her. It had milky white eyes and dry, cracked skin. Until suddenly, its scales cracked apart and a smooth, refreshed snake crawled out, leaving behind its skin.

She placed this too into the bowl. "A mare's hoof" was more difficult to come about. But it did so happen that her neighbor was a farmer. Draping herself in a dark, hooded cloak, and taking the bowl under her arm, Hortense dashed outside into the night. She scoured the field, finding cows, chickens, and pigs, before finally coming across a mare. Steadily, she approached the horse, not knowing what it would do, but to her surprise the mare extended her hoof, seeming to know exactly what the girl had planned.

With a smile, Hortense took the hoof in hand and placed it gently into the bowl. She stirred the skin and the milk, and just like her snakes said, the skin became plump and fresh. Hortense didn't look forward to what she needed to do next, but she had come this far. Taking the bowl to her lips, and after many moments of hesitation, she choked down the milk and moistened skin.

It slithered down her throat like a living snake. She felt sick. This had to be the most disgusting thing she had ever done. How desperate was she? After bidding the mare a green-faced farewell, she hurried home.

The next morning felt like any other. She crawled out of her bed, and besides the lingering aura of queasiness, she didn't have any immediate memory of what she had done.

But soon an unfamiliar image quickly brought the reality of it all rushing back. Crossing a mirror, she didn't see the cringe-inducing form she was used to, but a pretty, slender young girl. Her figure—instead of boxy and shapeless—was now elegantly thin. This was enhanced by smooth, dark hair caressing her face with a flattering shine.

"It worked," she breathed.

For the first time in her life, Hortense couldn't wait to leave her room. She dressed with pride, tightening her now loose dress with ribbons. Her parents seemed stunned at the quick glimpse they caught of her as she ran past. If her new appearance or her unbridled smile surprised them more, Hortense couldn't say. But she was sure that they were relieved to see her so happy for once, whatever the cause.

At school, Hortense received more attention than usual, which meant of course that she was getting any at all. In fact, it was as if people were looking at her for the first time. Boys and girls watched her with mixed looks of enticement and envy as she passed by in the halls; teachers called on her more in class, and some people even stopped to talk to her.

"Um, hello," said Emile, a skinny boy who had sat next to her in her music class for the past year.

"H-hi." Hortense's throat caught. She wasn't used to talking to boys. Especially ones who talked to her first.

"I was wondering if I could...um...borrow some of your notes?"

"...for music?"

"Oh, no, um...I guess we didn't really take notes. I just wanted to say hello."

Hortense blushed deeply. A boy was going out of his way to talk to her. Her heart felt like it was dancing on clouds.

"My name is Emile," he continued. "What's yours?"

And just like that, her heart came crashing back down. She'd been next to him for the entire year, and he was just now noticing her? Because her hair was pretty? And her waist was slim? She was about to stomp his foot, but then an idea struck her. No one knew Hortense. Hortense was a stranger—a boring lump on the road. But people knew her now. Maybe this new girl she'd become didn't have to be Hortense. Her mind raced, and she thought of the wonderful snakes that everyone was so afraid of. They'd seen her when no one else did. Maybe she could draw strength from them—from the fear that caused them to be such outcasts.

"Ophidia," she smiled. "My name is Ophidia."

"Wow, that's a really pretty name," Emile sighed cheerfully. The two spoke to each other much more often after that. In fact, many people spoke to *Ophidia* after that. Her group of friends was growing like wild ivy. Mainly they were boys like Emile: skinny, scruffy hair, oddly shaped noses, voices they hadn't yet grown into. Not ugly, but not particularly attractive. The girls were mostly of the same note; however, there were a few now speaking to her that were slightly more attractive. Once they joined her patch, the boys seemed to detract their attention from Ophidia.

Marguerite had bright green eyes, and Amelie had sculpted cheekbones. Ophidia dwelled on their looks, escaping to any mirror she could find to compare herself. Her eyes were a dull gray, and her cheeks quite flat. She made her decision. That night, Ophidia collected another slip of snakeskin and put it into a bowl with pure white milk, an eyelash, and a dusting of the rouge she had been using to color her cheeks. As before, she took the bowl to the neighbor's mare and stirred the contents within until the skin was plump. This time, swallowing the potion seemed slightly less disgusting. Some things were just easier to do when one had a firmer belief in them.

The next day, Ophidia's eyes were a vibrant, pond-like green resting over proud cheekbones. This, of course, boosted her popularity once more. Although some questioned her sudden enhancements, most admired her for it. She had gone her entire life being unnoticed, and now everybody in the school knew her name. Alas, her joy didn't last forever. It wasn't long before she began to notice things again. Gabrielle's blonde hair, Dominique's freckles, Marie's height.

But whatever she found herself wanting, it wasn't difficult to attain. The snakes were only too happy to lend her their

skin. They had become partners in crime of sorts to her. As for the rest, some milk here, mare's hoof there, tear drops, footprints, strands of hair, and drops of blood—all of these aided her as she weaved her spells.

One morning, as she was leaving for school and enjoying the new shape of her lips, she passed her mother and father chatting in the kitchen.

"Oh!" her mother gasped.

Noticing her mother's surprised expression, Ophidia realized it had been quite a while since she had actually seen her parents in the past few weeks beyond just quick passes throughout the house. Ophidia felt a swell of pride. She entered the kitchen so that her parents could take in all that she had accomplished throughout this time. She smiled, waiting for the compliments to come raining in.

"Hortense?" her father whispered after a long breadth of hesitation. "What have you done to yourself?"

Ophidia's smile dropped. This wasn't the praise she'd been waiting for. And that name...*Hortense*. It'd been so long since she'd heard it that it set off an unusual feeling. Ophidia felt a surge of disgust flow through her. "What have I done? I made myself beautiful."

"You've changed so much," her mother warbled. "I can barely recognize you."

Why weren't her parents happy for her? She'd finally become something she could be proud of. But they just kept looking at her with eyes full of worry and sadness and...*pity*?

"Hortense..." her mother began.

There it was again. *That name.* She never wanted to hear that name again! Her green eyes filled with fire as she clenched her chiseled jaw and rounded her fists.

"How dare you!"

Her parents moved to comfort her, but Ophidia spun quickly on her heel and darted out the door, tears streaming. Her parents were too small-minded for her. This town was too small-minded. If Ophidia was to become who she was truly meant to be, she needed room to grow. And that wasn't here.

Years passed. In Paris, a woman became known for the miracles she created. She could heal small ailments and tell your fortune, yes, but her true talents laid in the ability to transform. This woman could make anyone appear as they would in their wildest dreams. People came from all across the world to seek her help. As for how she appeared herself, well, no one could really tell you. She changed her face as one would change their clothes. Some days, the woman's most noticeable feature were her eyes—like those of a tiger's. Other days, her hair was streaked in pur-

ple and green and grew in loops around her head. Sometimes, her skin was dotted with specks of gold and silver. Her name? Ophidia, the Snake Woman.

One day, as Ophidia sat in her highly decorated office just overlook- ing the river, an old couple walked through the door. They were treated to the sight of her sprawled com- fortably across a lavish couch of pillows and surrounded by hanging lanterns of gold and crimson. Snakes slithered on windowsills and inside wicker baskets in corners of the room. Ophidia's lips were a deep black and as plump as ripe grapes; her metallic silver hair was tall with curls adorning one side; and her eyes shimmered with gold and red, no doubt to match her decor.

"Welcome," Ophidia said behind a smile of long, dazzling white teeth.

"Hello..." the old man said nervously. He had a ridiculously square face and an ugly, dimpled chin. She could see fear in his dull brown eyes. "Are you the...the Snake Woman?"

"I think her name is *Ophidia*, dear," the old wife whispered through gaudy red lips. She brushed back her tackily curled hair as she smiled at Ophidia, though she awkwardly avoided eye contact.

"Oh, yes, um, are you the woman they call Ophidia?"

"I am." Ophidia's words fell out of her mouth like a slithering snake. "What can I do for you today?" She reached for her milk-filled basin on the round table before her.

"We heard you can know a person's fortune...?"

"Oh." Ophidia trailed her hand back to her side. *How boring,* she thought. "I can indeed."

"We..." the wife began. "We were wondering if you could help us find someone?"

Ophidia flashed a fake smile and gestured to the slightly less extravagant couch across from the round table. The couple slowly approached it and sat down.

"Who is it that you seek?"

The woman pulled out an old photograph from her purse. It had clearly been handled too many times. The edges were all worn, and the print was heavily cracked. Ophidia extended her unusually long limbs and coiled her smooth fingers around the photo. She focused her flashing eyes on the image.

It was a girl. Ophidia's sweeping eyelashes widened as she scanned the girl's appearance. Such a unique figure, and hair like warm ash which wrapped about her head as if it were a bramble of roses. Her pale skin nearly mirrored the classical gray of her eyes, which were enhanced by the smooth shape of her face. Ophidia could certainly pick some features from this girl—perhaps even for tomorrow's visage.

"It's our daughter," the old man wheezed. "It's been years since we've seen her."

"We've tried everything to find her," the woman continued. "And then we heard of you...."

"We'll pay anything!" the man jumped in.

Ophidia looked up from the photograph with interest and gave the couple a wide smile. She laid the image on the table before them. "Well, it appears that you're in luck. This truly will be quite a simple search. Let me just consult my stones." She reached for a velvet bag on her belt and blew a breath into it through her black lips.

She shook the bag lightly, closing her eyes as she listened to the rattling as she would words. A confused expression rose across her unusual features. She opened her eyes and looked at the couple, who were looking back at her in anticipation.

"The stones are being rather playful today," she chortled. "Let's try this once more."

Ophidia rattled the bag again, more vigorously this time, and then drew it open, expelling the stones all across the table. They scattered over the photograph, around candles and crystals, and towards the old couple who watched on with bated breath. But an unusual thing happened as the stones came to a stop. They rattled again back across the table, tumbling into Ophidia's lap. She looked aghast at the stones. The old couple was quiet, their wide eyes glued to the witch.

Ophidia looked at the stones for a good long while, sitting comfortably on her embroidered dress. Finally, she looked back at the photograph on the table and took it once more into her smooth fingers. She knew who the girl was. Looking up from the image, with tears swelling behind her eyes, she stared at the old couple. The Snake Woman opened her mouth to speak, but her eyes shot quickly to a mirror beside the table as she caught a reflection of herself. She looked again onto the photograph and returned it to its place on the table, sliding it towards the old couple.

"I'm sorry," Ophidia said in a somber tone, choking back emotion. "Your daughter is dead."

Dandy's Dictum

Blackguard Slim was an awful man just as his name suggests;
Men dragged folks out from their own homes at his dark behest.
To the gallows, to the stakes, and to the iron box,
Many witches met their ends from Blackguard and his flocks.
"We don't curse, we only heal!" these witches would implore,
Though Blackguard Slim would just retort: "You're rotten at your core."
These witches sought to stand their ground, as only they knew how,
With love and light, though soon they found that Blackguard would not bow.
Now Dandy Duly healed well too, the best in all the land,
But this one witch thought it wise to cast with both his hands.
He slipped a peach from out his stores, and Blackguard took a bite,
Yet bitter as it was inside with maggots, mold, and fright!
His innards churned, his veins went dark, and bones turned into dough;
Then Dandy Duly came upon and shook his head in woe.
"You have done this to yourself. My fruit shows what is true;
And now it seems that all too clear, the rotten one is you!"
With this, the witch left Blackguard to wither into paste,
Though other witches righteously would turn their heads in haste.
"You've sullied our good name," they said. "We witches only heal!"
Dandy Duly then replied, "I've promised no such deal.
Your dictums are your own and this I'll never shun.
But left or right, I know mine too is 'do what must be done.'"

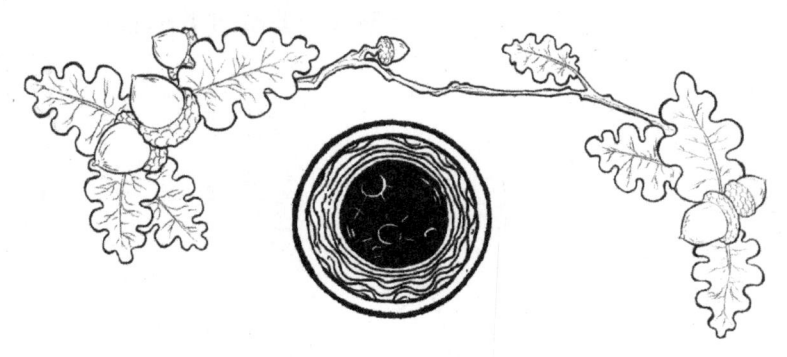

Chapter Eight

Behind White Lace

Down by the flatlands, where swamps gathered and rivers ran, stood a humble town known by the locals as Allium. The people there were sturdy, as they would have to be to stand the swamp's bitingly cold winters and the suffocating heat that followed in summer. A railway shot through the prairies of Allium like the barrel of a gun, splitting the cobbled roads of man and wild webs of the swamp. Most people of proper living didn't find themselves crossing the rails too often if they knew what was good for them.

Now, these parts were hard, and times were harder. Some folk had to sell the heat off their breath just to make ends meet. In winter, snow covered the prairies like a layer of wool, and even dropped change wouldn't be seen again until spring.

Nestled in this miserable frost was a dollop of a boy, no older than the sprig of a sassafras. He lived with his mother, whose cloud of dark hair matched his own, but where her eyes were like burnt amber, his were the color of warm chocolate fresh from the oven.

"Felix!" Momma yelled from the window of her small shack. "Come inside, boy, before you catch your death!"

The boy stood outside in the snow, bundled up in a patchy but thick jacket and long, oversized leather boots. His eyes were fixed on something in a nearby tree, and his ears seemed to be as well with all the attention he paid to his mother's hollering.

"Felix?" Momma came shuffling out into the cold, a thick wool blanket wrapped about her shoulders. "You got frost in your boots? Come inside!"

"Look, Momma," Felix whispered, his chocolate eyes as round as dinner plates. He pointed up to a high branch in the old hickory tree. There, upon one of its snow-covered limbs, sat a squirrel, black as charcoal, similar to a spot of ink on a fresh sheet of paper.

"You mind tellin' me why this rodent is at fault for me standin' in the snow?" Momma asked with tired eyes and a hidden smirk.

"It's a black squirrel, Momma!" Excitement rose in Felix's voice like a tea kettle. "Folks says that they're magic!"

"Oh, a magic rodent, then, is it? Well, I don't suppose your black squirrel can conjure up some clean dishes, then? Or better yet, get you inside before I need to tell you again?" Momma nudged Felix back towards the house, a little more of her smile creeping out from the corners of her rosy lips. "Now, *that* would be some magic I'd like to see."

"But Momma!" Felix whined, slouching his way to the shack. "Don't you 'but Momma' me! Go on, now, git!"

The squirrel sat, stable to the branch, its glossy eyes looking on in curiosity as the two jostled their way back into the house and shut the door behind them. The outside of their small home was humble as a box of rocks, and the inside was no different. Nothing but the bare necessities covered the rustic white walls, and a tiny hearth sputtered behind them.

Felix rushed through the front, toppling his boots and jacket into a heap on the floor. Momma shook her head exhaustedly as she followed behind him, picking up his mess.

"I love you, boy, but you could put a twister out of work," she groaned.

Felix reached into the pantry box for a hardening slice of old bread. Momma, with all the swiftness of a cottonmouth, slapped his hand away and gave him a glare.

"But, Momma, I'm hungry!"

"We don't got much, Buttah Bean. Gotta make this morsel last 'til we can get more."

"When's that?"

A sad shadow moved over Momma's eyes. "Well, with this winter as it is..." She looked down to Felix, innocent as an acorn cap, and smiled. "Well, never you mind that."

Felix settled his gaze on Momma for a bit, somewhat distracted from the low grumble of his stomach. "We don't got no money left to eat?"

Momma's neck tensed in surprise to her boy's words, but she eased herself back into a warm smile. "Let me worry about all that, Buttah Bean. You just keep smilin'."

"But what about you, Momma?"

Momma's smile widened to mask the water in her eyes. She lifted her left hand, the fourth finger extended like a warm day towards Felix. "D'you see this finger? This finger is made for promises. And I promise I'ma do just fine." She kissed it and gave her son a wink. "Now, you promise me that you're always gonna stay my happy little boy, you hear?"

Felix's face widened into a smile as he extended his own fourth finger, kissed it, and gave a wink back to his mother.

"Well, that's that." She nodded, patting down her apron. "Get to practicin' your letters, then, Felix. I've got a house to clean."

"Well, I can't be a happy boy if I gotta learn my letters!"

"Ah-ah-ah." Momma wagged her fourth finger. "A promise is a promise."

Felix's heavy pout twisted into a forced smile. Momma gave an amused nod of approval, and the boy mechanically took a ratty journal from the counter. With his pinned-up smile, he begrudgingly copied down words that Momma had previously written for him. As time went on, though, the words eventually turned into doodles, and the doodles into dreams.

One night, when the snow was coming down like wads of cotton and wind shook the little shack to its rafters, Momma stayed up late, feeding whatever she could into the hearth to keep it aglow. Felix laid in fragile torpor just the next room over. A gentle rapping came at the door. It was old Nora, a nearby neighbor with a cap covered in a thick layer of snow and a sack tucked firmly under her arm. She would oft come by on nights like these to share the hearth and feed it with some kindling of her own. Momma was all the more grateful for this on particularly cold nights, as that's when old Nora would come by with a bottle of whiskey tucked into her tinder pouch.

"You heard about the Granger boy? Little Curtis, I think it was," Nora sighed, taking another swig of her drink.

"Can't say I have," Momma said, lowering herself into a chair after throwing another slab of wood onto the fire.

"Sad, sad story." Nora shook her head. "They says he went missin' few days back."

"Oh, lord, no. Run away, did he?"

"If'n he did, I can't think about how he must be facing the cold. I can only pray he don't suffer."

Momma sipped on her cup, shaking her head. "Oh, his poor, poor parents."

"Least you got little Felix over there, tucked safely away."

Momma's brow furrowed. "I don't know if 'safe' is the right word." She let out a deep sigh, and her voice began to waver. "Not sure how we gonna make it this winter. Money's scarce, and food's scarcer."

"Sweetheart, it's hard for all of us. If I had any to spare...."

"I know, Nora. I'm not askin' for nothin'." Momma sat silent for a moment and took a long gulp of her drink. "Maybe the Grangers are better off."

"You don't mean that, now."

"One less mouth to feed. A least they don't got no more reason to worry."

Nora sat in silence. She leaned forward with her bottle of whisky and poured Momma another glass. "You need this more than I do, girl."

It might have been the snow sliding from the roof or the clap of the shudders sparring against the wind that did it, but Felix had awoken from his slumber quite some time ago. The walls of the shack were not as thick as the whisky had convinced the women they were, either. He sat there, trying to take in all that he'd heard. There was much that he didn't understand, but one thing he was sure of: Momma would be better off without him.

The two women continued to chatter, drink, and feed the hearth. He couldn't hear anything else they said, though, as Momma's words rang too loud in his ears. What was he going to do now? Felix huddled up under his white nightshirt for warmth—or maybe just to catch his tears.

The wind was bustling something fierce outside. He was sure the walls would come crashing down. It all just seemed to be getting louder and louder. Momma and old Nora didn't seem bothered by it, but Felix felt like he was being surrounded by hungry bears. It grew more and more violent by the moment. The room itself seemed to be shaking. And then, right across from him, the window slowly creaked open amidst thrashing winds.

Sitting just there, in the frosty white darkness, an inky figure waited for him. The black squirrel. It stared at the boy, eerily still, the snow and wind dying away from it like wilting blades of grass.

The boy slowly moved towards the squirrel. When they were just inches from each other, it turned and lept away from the snow-shrouded windowsill. As it did, wind burst through the opening, choking Felix with the cold. Snow-flakes began to collect on his dark patch of hair.

The squirrel turned to look at him again, a pristine white valley spread out around its feet. Felix took a deep breath, the cold stinging his lungs, and jumped through the low window. He let out a yelp as he sunk into the snow up to his thighs. But he couldn't hear his own voice, much less his thoughts in the squall that spun around him.

Slowly, Felix made his way through the banks of ice. With every step, he could feel his skin a little less. It felt like he was wading through frozen molasses to reach the squirrel. Finally, as he came up to the creature, his feet seemed to hit solid ground. The winds swerved to avoid him, and he felt placidly warm. Now, instead of wading through the snow, he—with the squirrel—was standing on top of it as if he was as weightless as a maple seed.

The squirrel turned and began to prance away again from the boy. Feeling the cold slowly creep up on him again, Felix chased after it. He jostled close behind, watching its black tail bobbing over the pearly snow. Everything was so still and quiet around him. He began to wonder whether time itself had frozen in the cold.

The prairie was vast and white as a lake of cream. He ran and ran to keep up with the critter, but not once did he feel tired or strained. His bare feet actually felt nice on the soft cushion of snow. This had to be what it was like to dance on clouds.

Soon enough, the pair found themselves bounding up to that unmistakable line in the snow. No matter how deep the winter, it seemed that the railroad still struck the land, clear as a rip in a pair of trousers. But as he hung to the squirrel's pace, that line was quickly crossed, and with it, all the burdens of Allium were left behind. He felt a twinge of guilt, but under that, a bellow of glee.

Trees began to busy their path. The forest thickened, and the night grew darker still as Felix and his squirrel companion waltzed on into the woods. If it weren't for the bright snow, he was sure he wouldn't be able to make his nose out in front of his face.

Naked trees stretched and gnarled all around them. Icicles clung to their branches like colonies of bats. The squirrel was surefooted in stitching this maze, though, and Felix found it best just to follow. He was too far gone from home now and knew that if he gained too much distance from the critter, this winter would swallow him whole.

Eventually, the snowy floor faded to ice. While the cold still couldn't touch him, the ground no longer felt like clouds beneath his feet. *These gotta be them swamps that everyone's always whisperin' about,* Felix thought. He knew that this was a place he was not supposed to be.

Felix had seen darkness before, but looking upon the frozen swamps, he felt he was seeing something that he shouldn't. The land had an ancient and predatory air about it. It was like death itself had laid down and become the very stones on which he stood. Yet, there was something alluring about it too. Like a sweet mystery beckoning him to stay longer, come closer, and give in.

The two reached a clearing over the ice where the trees yawned apart as if to mime some kind of nest or gnarled pit. The squirrel slowed to a stop, as did Felix. He waited patiently for the squirrel to continue on, but it only stood there, waiting.

All at once, Felix's wear caught up with him as if it were running just a few paces behind, waiting for him to slow. The boy drooped over the ice, trying to catch himself before he fell and cracked like an egg. The darkness around him grew blacker still, and before he knew it, Felix drifted into a deep sleep.

In what felt like the span of a sigh, Felix found himself squinting into a bright wall of sunlight. A confused haze filled his head like a cloud of June bugs as he blinked into the blinding glare. The light eventually eased itself to reveal bare trees arching overhead and a glassy sheet of ice beneath.

The dark frame of the black squirrel stepped into view, and the haze quickly left Felix's mind. His chocolate eyes widened as feelings of fear and fervor wrestled in the back of his throat. He sat upright with a gasp to take in the display of lukewarm permafrost that surrounded him. Yet as his sight settled, an even more unusual vision filled his eyes.

There, in the frozen bog, nestled between trees where just last night not even foxtails grew, stood an old and elegant manor. It was a perfect picture of white, even purer than the snow that surrounded it. White-sided walls, a white picket fence, and a white stone trail, which slithered up its way to the front door. Delicate pearly lace cascaded from every window and along the countless drying lines that ran from the house to the surrounding trees.

It seemed nearly untouched by the swamp, as if nature and the manor both refused to accept the others' existence. The only sign of these worlds intermingling at all was from frosted briar vines stretching out along the corners of the home to the rigid fence posts at the property's edge—though it was unclear if these too were sprouting from the spectral home.

With a haunting groan, the wooden door creaked open. The squirrel turned its head, entranced by the figure emerging from the opening. A slender, elderly woman stood there, draped in a long dress woven of fine lace, even dandier than that which decorated the manor. It covered her from her neck to her toes and then some, trailing further behind her. Her face, too, was hidden behind a beautifully pale woven veil. She was an embodiment of the mystery that surrounded the house, wizened and elegant.

The woman slowly and gracefully began to move forward as if she were gliding through water. As she left the beckoning shadows of her threshold, the squirrel scampered quickly away in her direction. Felix felt the cold of the frozen floor quickly rush up on him like the snap of a whip. He scurried to his feet, trying to get as much of himself off the ice as possible, but it didn't do him a lot of good. Where the cold wasn't gripping its claws into his bare feet, it was biting his skin through the ceaseless air. He rattled like a string of bones in the wind, and as his eyes darted up to find the magical squirrel, he saw the old woman standing just a mere foot away from him at the end of her stone trail.

"Well, look at you, sweet one," the woman spoke in a soft but muffled voice, as if she were hiding a bite of taffy in the corner of her mouth. A smile hung to her words like a disapproving humor. "Seems like you might have taken a wrong turn past the bedpost, hon."

Felix was shrinking into a ball, standing on the hem of his nightshirt to try and separate himself from the ice. "Th-the squirrel t-took me here...."

"Ah, yes, my pets have led quite the odd number of children to my stoop throughout the years. Seems there are many who they deem need a proper home." The old woman slowly extended her arm towards the boy. "Come. Come, sweet pea. You are welcome in my manor."

Felix stared blankly at her long fingers stretching out towards him as the fog from his breath began to dwindle.

"Come now, my honeycomb. Before you go bluer than the hoarfrost. That's no color for little children."

Felix let a smile lift his frozen cheeks with a sharp pang. The boy reached out and grabbed her hand. The two slowly made their way up the winding trail to the old manor. Felix's skin stung as it finally hit warm air. He rattled like an aspen leaf on the floor of the house's foyer. The woman glided past him as if she were mist on the wind.

"Here, my sweet. For the shivers." She held out her hand to him; in it sat a deep, red plum. "It will help, I promise."

Felix took the plum and bit into it. Sweetness bloomed across his tongue, and as it did, he suddenly felt the chill leave his bones. His warmth was quickly returning and so too did the movement in his arms and legs. The boy excitedly took another bite of the red fruit but found the second taste to be downright foul. He must have been making a disgusted face because the old woman relieved him of the fruit.

"Has it gone bad?" she sighed. "This winter has not treated my plums kindly, I fear. I do find that the sweetest things tend to turn the most bitter."

"It's okay." Felix smiled. "Least I'm warm now!" The boy took the chance now to blink the daze out of his eyes and take his first look around the peculiar manor. Its insides did not match its outsides. In fact, its insides did not match any house that he had ever seen before.

Many thin staircases and dainty lofts crisscrossed through the home from the floor to high ceiling, connecting to several rooms, each on their own level, and each with doors of different shapes. Some parts of the house seemed older than the rest, each section changing slightly in style and make. It was like a circus of time, evolving from hall to hall and wall to wall.

The squirrel that had been Felix's guide chittered from the witch's feet to a scurry of others that sat on a high loft.

"Do you know what makes them so special?" the woman asked, picking up the dark critter.

Felix lowered his attention towards the squirrel. "Uh...I heard they was magic?"

"Yes...and no. You see, the squirrels are drawn to magic like bees to honey. Yet it is only the ones that truly *believe* in magic that the squirrels will permit to follow." Felix's eyes lit up as his heart fluttered to her words. "Do *you* believe in magic, my boy?"

"Mm-hmm!"

"Ah, wonderful. Would you like to learn how to *use* magic?"

A bright smile stretched out across his rosy cheeks. "Yes! Are *you* magic?"

"My dear, yes. I am the raggedy old witch of these briars. Though you, little one, may address me as Nonna Noxa."

Felix was glowing with joy. He couldn't believe it. His frosty brush with death had almost been forgotten at this point. The lace-draped woman turned her back to him and slowly began to move further into the web, drifting like a pedal on the surface of a pond. She beckoned him to follow with her long, knobby finger.

The boy trotted along behind her as if he were an excited puppy. The black squirrel sat on the witch's shoulder, watching him with a finely pointed interest.

"You should first meet the others, I think," the witch said.

"There's others?"

"Yes, others like yourself! Children who have followed the squirrels."

"Are they friendly?"

"Well, yes. Though some have been on hard times. But once they sense a kindred spirit, I'm sure they will appreciate meeting such a sweet thing like you."

Felix puffed out his chest to this. He walked along with the silent wading of Nonna Noxa's steps. Felix examined all sorts of things lined along the walls—none of which he could read the labels on, of course. He imagined them to be many unusually witchy things: jars of tars, vials of biles, and boxes of poxes. These thoughts bubbled and tickled in his mind until he noticed the slithering train of Nonna Noxa's dress come to a stop. Looking forward, he saw the white-laced witch standing before a lancet door.

A ball of knots clumped together in the boy's throat. What would magical kids be like? Were they fun or mysterious or larger than life? He suddenly felt very silly standing there in nothing but a woolen nightshirt.

The door swung open, and Nonna Noxa ushered the boy in. The room smelled of rust and the day after a heavy rain. Eleven other children filled the dimly lit corners of the

space, each slowly waking from their drab little beds. Felix felt the witch's eight long fingers wrap themselves around his shoulders as she presented him to the lot.

"Good morning, children," she began in her muffled voice. "I would like to introduce you to our newest friend here." There was a resounding silence in response to the witch's announcement and most certainly nary a smile. "Well...best of luck, little one," the witch said with a knowing sympathy. "A new set of clothes is in the wardrobe. I do think you will fit right in here."

Nonna Noxa turned around and closed the door behind her as she left. The boy slowly worked his gaze about the dank room. At a glance, Felix appeared to be the youngest of the bunch, while the eldest of the children was nestled somewhere in the midst of her gangly teens. Many of the group wore expressions in daze and distraction, but a good few seemed almost ill and downright dismal. Their skin even had a clammy green tint to it as they sneered bullets in Felix's direction.

He wondered how anyone learning magic could be so bitter. Had he made a mistake leaving home? Just then, he felt a warm tingle. Felix's eyes dropped to the fourth finger of his left hand, and he was reminded of the promise he made to his mother. *Promise me that you're always gonna stay my happy little boy.* With more bravery than he thought he had, he mustered a smile. This caught the attention of another boy who was probably the closest in age to Felix. Although he didn't seem near to mustering up a smile of his own, he also didn't appear quite as soured as the others.

"Hello!" Felix chirped at the boy. His voice seemed to reverberate against the deafening silence of the others, and was, of course, returned with more snide glares.

"Oh...hi," the boy spoke quietly as he made brief eye contact with Felix through his thick, round glasses. He was pale with a thin neck balancing a round head, which reminded Felix of a dandelion.

"I'm Felix! What's your name?"

"...Curtis," the dandelion boy let half a smile escape as he gave Felix another glance. Felix met this, of course, with an even wider grin.

Well, the following days passed with the ease of an uphill river. The witch, behind her white lace, said that the circle would convene when the moon went dark. After that, she was rarely seen roaming about the manor at all. Felix would catch sight of her train rounding a corner and maybe hear her warm, muffled voice lilting through the halls on occasion. Yet no one knew where she would disappear to when the night went black.

In the meantime, each child was assigned their chores. The oldest children had the easiest chores, though they seemed the more miserable despite it. One girl was in charge of sweeping snow while a boy made sure that all the laundry lines stayed dry.

For Curtis and Felix, however, the chores were much more rigorous. Curtis would need to clean the coals and the chimney from the hearth, though the fire was rarely extinguished for him to accomplish this. Felix's job was to push nails into the floor without having been given anything besides his bare hands with which to do it. At least he had the squirrels to keep him company. One of them seemed to take a particular liking to him and would often sit on his shoulder as he worked.

One day, when Curtis returned smudged and cindered, Felix had just finished a line of nails. His fingers were swelling something fierce, like the ripe plums Nonna Noxa fed them at supper. Curtis drudged across the hall, his eyes red with tears as he looked over his friend's poor fingers.

"Wow..." said Felix in somber awe. "Ya look like the wrong end of a raven."

"Yeah?" Curtis narrowed his eyes at the boy and pointed to his swollen fingers. "Better the wrong end of a raven than the underside of a cow."

The two glowered at each other for the breath of a moment before immediately bursting out into laughter. The squirrel on Felix's shoulder flinched at this sudden sound which so rarely danced in these halls, but they didn't care. They were both tired, both blistered, and both beyond reason at this point.

"How is it that you have more nails to push every day?" Curtis wondered, wiping a tear from his soot-stained cheek.

Felix shrugged, "I dunno. Figured the cold mighta had somethin' to do with it."

"Well, I would gladly take more cold in my chores if you had any to spare."

"I got pockets of cold! Have as much as ya want!"

The two broke out into giggles again until footsteps rounded the corner. It was the eldest of the children, a tall knobbly girl whose skin had the sheen of mold and the viscous touch of a toad.

"What have you roaches to laugh about?" she sneered.

Curtis's smile fell as hastily as his gaze as he stared down at his feet. "Um...nothing, Genevieve."

"Nothing? Well, I've got something for you to laugh about. Look at you, all covered in ash. You're like something I left in the outhouse. Aren't you?" She stared at the boy for a moment before her sneer curled even deeper. *"Aren't you?"*

"Y-yes."

"Yes what?"

"Yes, I-I'm like something you l-left in the outhouse."

The girl's sneer shifted into a cruel smirk. "There. Now isn't that funny?"

Curtis nodded, his eyes welling up with tears. Felix cringed, feeling his friend's joy float away, like his dandelion down was spiraling off into the wind.

"You ain't half as funny as you think," he growled.

Genevieve's glare slowly crawled to the corner of her eye as she looked down on Felix. The girl towered over him, at

this moment seeming twice her height. Like a flash of lightning, she swung her hand upwards across Felix's face. The squirrel sprung off him quickly before the boy thudded hard onto the ground.

The girl kept her glare sharply on him through the corner of her eye, as if looking at him straight on would cause a stack of books to fall from her head.

"You ain't even worth my time, roach." The boys watched in confusion as she then bit down hard onto her own tongue and said:

> "Singing iron like a kettle's spout,
> Wake from your beds and out, out, out!"

With this, the girl spat her blood onto the floor and walked rigidly out of the room.

Felix and Curtis exchanged faces of pain and dismay, but all of a sudden, a stinging whistle filled the hall. The boys tracked their eyes to the source of the sound. The floor nails that Felix had spent his days pushing in began to vibrate. One of them slowly shook its way out of the floor and clattered flat onto the board. This was followed by the next one and the next until one by one, all of Felix's work had been undone.

The boy lay there on the ground, his face burning and his throat tight. Like Curtis, tears began to fill his eyes. The dandelion boy drooped down to Felix, helping him up to his feet.

"That awful Genevieve. I *hate* her!" Curtis growled.

"Don't say, that. She might hear ya and come back."

Curtis stiffened at this, biting his lip. "Well...do you want me to help you put them back in?"

"Naw," Felix sighed, getting down on his knees. "It's okay...."

Curtis watched on for a moment as Felix twisted the nails back into place. "Alright...." The boy slowly made his way down the hall, watching Felix over his shoulder.

Times like these were the hardest in the manor, but not all too rare. Still, through it all, Felix wore his smile like a warm coat on a winter's night. And when he forgot, as he often would, his fourth finger would tingle and put him right again. Even when it bled from his labor, it would always remind him to smile.

Finally, the day of the dark moon arrived. The children were all gathered into a room off one of the staircases that threaded through the house. For this, they needed to be washed and dressed in their new clothes. Boys wore jackets and trousers while the girls wore high-collared dresses—all dotted with copper buttons, all woven in Nonna Noxa's fine silk, dyed gray like smoke.

The room itself was odd, which didn't say much in a house like this, but odd all the same. The walls reflected like tarnished silver that had sat in the back of a cupboard for too long. Pronged sconces stretched out as if they were greedy hands, each giving off their own feeble light. This made it hard to see, and Felix felt like he had stepped into a room made of dusk. In the center of the space stood a massive, round table. With a closer read, Felix could see that it too was reflective, though instead of silver, it was made of something like black glass.

Nonna Noxa suddenly glided into the room like a pregnant silence, the door closing shortly behind her long train. Her white lace glowed like a misty morning against the dark shade of the room. The children who drifted about the space suddenly settled into their places around the table as the witch gestured them near.

"Hello, my plums," the witch's voice chimed. While her face remained veiled, a warm smile poured through the lace. "The moon has brought us much magic tonight. Now, tell me. Who wants to work a little witchcraft?"

Felix nodded like a screw was loose on the hinge of his neck, and even Curtis couldn't hide his excitement. A few of the other children raised their eyes in anticipation while some took a nervous gulp. The greenest of the children didn't react at all, and in fact, stood steadfast as if trying to hold their place against a train barreling towards them.

Nonna Noxa reached into her sleeve and pulled out a thin, pointed vial filled with what seemed to be liquefied algae. She reached out over the children, and with her spindly arm, held it above the table like a railroad spike about to be plunged into the earth. She pressured her thumb down over a switch on top of the vial. The algae-like ooze trickled through the end of the pointed glass, and three drops fell into the yawning center of the table.

The witch replaced the vial into her sleeve, and a squelch-like sound could nearly be heard from behind her veil. Suddenly, she spoke. This time, however, her voice was different. There was a rhythm to it, much the same as a storyteller might have. She leaned into the children and began to speak with great movement in her arms, as if weaving a tale:

> *"Who sits atop their silver thrones?*
> *Whose robes are sewn,*
> *Of precious stones,*
> *And built on mounds of others' bones?*
>
> *Who might it be, the ne'er-do-well?*
> *What soul could tell,*
> *Whose eyes befell,*
> *Or knew whereby their stead may dwell?*
>
> *This is the query that grew ever wider,*
> *It troubled the court and all the outsiders.*
> *The king asked the queen, and the queen asked the rider,*
> *The rider his horse, and the horse to the spider.*
>
> *The spider she knew, and she spun in her lace.*
> *With golly and grace,*
> *Her fingers did race,*
> *And fashioned the form of the ne'er-do-well's face."*

The witch's dancing hands stilled as her final words rang in the air. She pointed one long fingernail up to the ceiling and then brought it down onto the glass. From her touch, a piercing, tinny ring chimed through the room. This sent shivers down Felix's spine, which felt like snakes wriggling their way through his bones, into the shimmering black table.

Another silent squelch sounded from behind the white lace veil. The old woman's gaze broke its dead focus and peered about the table to each of the children. With a return to her warm voice, she addressed the group.

"My sweet ones, this magic that I am about to teach you is powerful. I hope that it will do you much good in the future if you mean to use it wisely." She placed her hand upon the table and caressed its surface as if it were a prized horse. "Look here upon the glass. Think of your betters. Those who claim to outstand you in every way. In beauty, intelligence, or class. These wicked souls would no sooner smile for your feats than they would mourn for your corpse.

Well, we shall not let that stand. With this most invaluable of spells, you, my darlings, may take from them the subject of their taunt." She gazed once more around the table at the children whose eyes sparkled with captivation. "Now, little ones, peer into the blackness, and may the faces of your oppressors appear to you."

Around the table, each child lost themselves into the blackness, their eyes becoming as glassy as its surface. For each of them, a face took form, though it was not seen by any, save for its onlooker. Before Felix appeared the face of Genevieve, who had tormented him all these days. He felt his blood twinge at the rancid sight of her.

"Good, my sweet ones, very good," Nonna Noxa chimed. "Now, swell that righteous fury forward. Of all that our bodies govern, tongues are the witch's most essential portion. Thus, you must build this fury, your venom, into your mouths. Once it has pooled behind your teeth, spit it down onto the vision. Do this, and what is theirs shall soon be yours."

One by one, the children began to spit onto the table. To no one's surprise, it was Genevieve who spat first. Her saliva landed on the table. It quickly turned a bloody red, then black, and then sizzled like water on a hot pan. The same occurred for each of the children.

Felix was nearly ready. He shot a quick look towards the cruel witchling girl, a satisfying smirk growing across his lips. Just as he was about to spit, though, he felt another tingle on his fourth finger. Satisfaction sunk hard in his chest. After a solemn pause, Felix took a deep breath and pursed his lips. Instead of spitting onto the table, he bent down and gave the vision a kiss.

The boy let out a sigh and felt the venom dissipate. Slowly, Felix drew himself back up and raised his sight from the table. His heart made a short jump at the sight of everyone staring at him. Nonna Noxa stood like a statue, still as stone, her veiled face frozen in his direction.

Felix's cheeks turned hot from embarrassment. Some of the children giggled at his expense or looked to the witch for further instruction. Despite himself, Felix felt himself crumbling under the weight of their snickering. He tried to gather more venom, but the vision had already disappeared, and no more fury pulsed through his small body. Sweat began to gather along the line of his short hair.

Like a crack in the ice, Nonna Noxa broke her stillness. She looked hastily around the circle and gave a short nod to the group.

"Well spelled, my plums. Continue to practice this magic and you will be a true witch just that much sooner." With this, she turned away. The door opened, and the witch quickly drifted from its silver walls.

The children slowly trickled from the room as well. Curtis looked to Felix and gave him a weak smile before leaving the room with the rest of the children. Felix moved to follow, but Genevieve crossed his path. She squinted her eyes, and a wicked smile cut her clammy face. The girl rose her hand as before to Felix, but just then, something changed. A shift of emotion brushed across her, and she lowered her hand. A furrow creased her brow, and the girl then too left the dark room.

The days carried on again as the children saw to their chores. Felix would pass Genevieve as he searched for nails, finding her shaking dust off the lace curtains. Unusually, she didn't sneer at him anymore, nor did her face appear quite as sickly green as before. In fact, one day, she even apologized after bumping into him. He wasn't sure what had gotten into her, but the boy wasn't about to start questioning it.

Felix also had less and less work to do. Soon, he wasn't able to find any loosened nails at all. His fingers were even beginning to return to their natural color. With all of this extra time, he figured he'd help Curtis with the hearth. The dandelion boy seemed to be losing his fluff quicker these days. Curtis was wearier, thinner, and paler than before. It didn't even matter how much Felix offered to help; Curtis resigned himself to begrudgingly take on his blistering task alone.

So, Felix returned to his hunt for loose nails. He wandered up nearly every staircase, over every loft, and through every hall, but though he searched, the ordeal seemed to have remedied itself. During one search, with his squirrel friend perched comfortably on his shoulder, Felix came to a door made of old, weathered wood, unevenly cobbled together. Compared to the patchwork of doors that littered the manor, this one was plain unsuspecting. Suspiciously unsuspecting, in fact.

With an overwhelming urge of curiosity, Felix tried the wooden latch, but it had been locked tight. With a disappointed sigh, the boy shrugged and began to wander again through the halls. As he made his distance, the squirrel jumped from Felix's shoulder and scurried its way back to the door. He chased after it, but just as the squirrel slowed before the ancient wood and Felix thought he'd cornered it, the door gingerly eased itself open. Without pause, the black squirrel pranced through the opening. Felix hesitated at the entrance, but it didn't take long to convince himself that it would be just irresponsible to not follow at this point.

The boy and his squirrel entered into an area with all the necessities of home. A table, an old hearth stove, hutches along the walls, and a cot in the corner. At

first glance, this room reminded Felix of his own home in Allium—though much, much older. In fact, this space seemed to be older than any other part of the manor, almost as if the rest of the home had simply been built around it over time.

He examined the varying jars that lined the hutch shelves. In one bottle, he swore he could see disembodied shadows moving about, while in another, enticing black berries not unlike possums' eyes were bunched together. A few small vials even stood on the central table, which the boy recognized as batches of Nonna Noxa's algae-green liquid. More than anything else, however, he could see plums. Baskets, jars, and boxes of plums. It seemed Felix had found Nonna Noxa's secret stash.

The squirrel, though, scurried past all of the curios that distracted Felix and followed a line like a scent through the shadows of the room. This drew the boy's attention, and he followed the small animal who came to a dead stop before a wrought iron pedestal. Upon this sat a sort of book, though that word hardly seemed enough to describe it.

Felix felt as though looking upon it, he was facing a bear that was beckoning him into its mouth. As reluctant as he was to it, he couldn't help but draw himself closer. The ivory-white cover was chalky and hard like bone. Still, the boy pressed further on. He opened the ribbed cover and slowly flipped through its silvery pages. Every word inside registered only as scratches of ink. Felix could hear his mother's voice in his head, telling him to learn his letters, and he groaned at how right she was.

The images, though, were too curious to simply ignore. Intricately lined drawings, like those that a doctor would keep, filled the pages. Many centered on the human tongue, though one section was splashed with a large illustration of a figure whose head, chest, and stomach were filled with a dark black substance.

With little hesitation, Felix darted around the room until he found a sheet of blank paper and a stray pen. With haste, the boy reconstructed what he could from the silver pages onto the paper. Though it was a sloppy copy, and the letters meant nothing to him now, he was determined to figure them out.

The next few days proved to be a challenge for the boy. His new interest distracted him from his fruitless task of searching for loose nails as he began to decipher his copied text. He began by learning letters from words that he already knew the meanings of. Felix learned S-A-L-T and P-E-P-P-E-R from the kitchen, C-O-A-L and M-A-T-C-H-E-S from boxes beside the hearth, and O-I-L from a couple lamps in the foyer. He asked Curtis for help, too, when the other was willing, but he brushed Felix off more often than not.

His friend seemed to turn greener and meaner with each passing sunrise. Some nights, Felix went to bed and found hot coals on his mattress. Other days, iron nails would appear in his porridge. Nails which he would, of course, need to push into the floor later wherever he found them missing. If there was any question, it was definite now that the dandelion boy had no fluff left.

Eventually, the moon grew full and faded again into darkness. The time had finally tarrived for the circle to convene once more. The room this time was small, and the children had to nearly huddle together to even fit inside. A striped wallpaper lined the walls, reminding Felix of bars. The witch stood in the center of the room like a warden clad in wistful white.

Felix looked around the assembly and noticed that Genevieve was not among them. He had neither seen her in the halls nor their dorm for days. Magic, however, was something he was sure that the lanky girl wouldn't want to miss. He wondered to himself why he should even care, but a tingle across his finger and a burning sense of curiosity pushed him forward. Timidly, Felix addressed the old witch standing among them.

"Nonna Noxa?"

The witch turned her veiled head towards the boy. "Yes, my peach?"

"I was wonderin' where Genevieve might have gone?" Some of the children tilted their ears towards this question, like they were wondering the same thing but didn't want to ask.

"Are you missing your friend, sweetie?"

The thought of Genevieve as a friend was enough to bring a cringe to Felix's lips. He could even hear a snort from one of the other children in the room. "Well, it's just 'cuz I ain't seen her in a while is all."

Nonna Noxa sighed, "It's true. Genevieve has gone. A fine witch, that girl."

"Gone? Where did she go?" one girl asked quietly. Felix had seen Genevieve once knot the girl's pigtails to a hot stove.

"It was simply time for her to leave us," the old woman replied. "There was nothing more I had to teach her. It will happen to you all one day, and I couldn't be prouder for it."

"What will she do now?" another child began, but Nonna Noxa held a hand up to him.

"Let's not speak any more of it for now. We've much magic to work before the moon begins to shine again. And this is an art I imagine you will each find very useful."

Felix's heart began to flutter, and he looked for Curtis, hoping to share in at least a spark of excitement. Upon spotting his friend, however, Curtis didn't pay him any mind. Yet, in the close confines of this room, Felix could see him clearer than he had in weeks. Curtis's pale skin had taken on a clammy green hue similar to Genevieve's. A shadow of concern wafted Felix's face, but he had to bite his tongue as the witch began.

Nonna Noxa reached into her drooping sleeve and uncovered the bright green vial from its depth. She pulled on her dress's long train, revealing that beneath it laid a bevy of white cloth swatches. Each swatch was paired with long silver pins, the kind fancy women would often stick into their hats. She held out the vial and pressed the switch. A drop fell onto the floor and slithered across like rain on a windowpane to one of the swatches of cloth. Nonna Noxa repeated this for each swatch, and with every drop, the liquid slithered down to be absorbed by the white material.

She gave a silent nod just as another squelch trickled from behind her veil. Leaning down to the level of the

children, Nonna Noxa started again to weave for them a tale in her rhythmic voice:

> *"The rats! The rats! All about scattered,*
> *The pantry is ravaged, the curtains are tattered,*
> *The laundry is savaged, the dishes are shattered,*
> *The rats! The rats! Everywhere spattered!*

> *But the serpent, she knew, how rats can be fickle,*
> *So when they slept, she snuck into their mickle,*
> *And down her fangs, a venom did trickle,*
> *With which would deliver a burn, itch, and tickle.*

> *Out with the rats! Out with their spats!*
> *Writhing and squealing onto the mats,*
> *Tumbling through the wide-open flats,*
> *And into the claws of the hungry field cats."*

Like an expert seamstress, Nonna Noxa threaded her tale, magic spinning into every word. The children hung onto her story like flies on honey. They could feel a pulse move among the air between them. The swatches of cloth, once still, suddenly began to throb upon the floor like beating hearts. With this, Nonna Noxa replaced the vial into her sleeve.

The witch's voice squelched back to normal, and she said, "Now listen close, my peaches. There will be matters in your life that may need to be subdued. For this, *binding* is a most essential art in every witch's arsenal. These spells will hold still that which may do you harm or otherwise disturb you. Do you understand?"

The children nodded about the circle. She appeared pleased at this and gestured the children towards the swatches. As each knelt before the cloths, she continued.

"Pull forth your witch's venom once more, children. Allow it to swell within your mouth. Let all that has held you back pour forth. Once the venom burns hot on your tongue, anoint the silver with its spite. When the pin is wet, pierce the cloth before you!"

Felix wondered what might need to be bound. He certainly felt disgruntled, but at what? His chores? Could he bind those? Or maybe these tight uniforms? Binding might have been the issue there, not the solution. Children around him were already wetting their pins. Curtis was the first, and when he was ready, he thrust his pin into the cloth.

It squirmed and thrashed as if it was trying to get away, but the silver pin kept the cloth tight in place. A stain of deep red spread across clean fabric from where the pin had punctured it. Eventually, the hostile cloth submitted and laid still. One after another, the other children enacted their spells, each with satisfying grins on their faces, and each met with similar thrashes and squirms.

Felix's tongue was beginning to grow hot. He drew the pin closer to his mouth and placed his other hand onto the material to keep it still. He could feel a pulse in its threads. It was like a living person. The cloth suddenly took shape in his eyes, as if it was draped over somebody, taking their form. It was Curtis! The thing holding him back was Curtis? Maybe this spell would bind him, and they could be friends again!

Felix was excited at the idea of regaining the dandelion boy. His tongue was now burning, and he placed the pin between his lips. Just then, as if on cue, his finger began to tingle. All of his excitement quickly melted into a sticky feeling of guilt. With that, the burning in his mouth suddenly turned placid and cool.

Felix let go of his spite, and with a sigh, kissed the tip of the pin. Instead of a violent jab, he placed it down over the cloth and hung his head in defeat. The cloth now, instead of squirming, slowly started to expand. Then, much like a chest, it let out the sound of a long, releasing breath and once again laid flat on the table.

A Witch's Book of Terribles

From under his disappointed eyebrows, Felix looked up at the circle. Everyone was once again staring at him. They were ready for his mistake this time and instantly burst into howls of laughter.

"He messed it up again!" one of the greener children chortled. "The cloth just farted at him!"

"He ain't got what it takes to be magic."

"We should get rid of him!"

The children all broke out into a chatter on how best to deal with Felix as Nonna Noxa attempted to calm them.

"Now, now," she said. "The best things come from patience. Felix has a magic all his own...."

Her anecdotes were muffled in the din of the crowd, though. Felix was so lost in dismay and embarrassment that he didn't notice Curtis leave the room. In fact, Curtis refused to even look at Felix after that day.

He was lucky, though, to at least still have the black squirrel by his side. At least it could keep him company as he continued to decipher the alphabet. He was getting good at it too. By now, he could sound out smaller words and even copy down the pages neatly.

When he could, he would sneak back into the strange room to write more from the book. He still wasn't sure about the content. He could make out something about sweetness, bitterness, and the use of a tongue. Felix was beginning to think he'd found a cookbook instead of a magic one.

Nonetheless, he worked hard. Momma would have been proud of him. He was proud of himself too. Every day after examining the manor for loose nails, Felix would go with his squirrel to a quiet corridor so that he could read. One day when there were particularly few nails to push in, he discovered something unusual in the text about two tongues. One tongue that spoke only with reason and one tongue that spoke only with rhyme. *If reason takes its rhyme, then the rhymes may lose all reason.*

"I don't think I wrote this right," Felix groaned, scratching his head. He rubbed the squirrel between its ears as it nibbled on a kernel of corn. "C'mon, scruff-butt. I gotta get more letters from that book."

Felix jauntily traversed the hallways. With his months of practice, he was now quite familiar with the manor and its nonsensical layout. Finally, he reached the secluded wooden door. It creaked slowly open, and the boy slid inside. With a small stack of papers in hand, he maneuvered his way through the shadowy room. The book lay upon the pedestal, waiting. He felt as though it was watching him, the way Momma did when she would call him in to tell him off.

With great reverence, he flipped through the silver pages to find the section about two tongues. Skimming the book, he came across a figure of the human form. Something about it caught his eye. The blackness filling the head, chest, and stomach began to change. It took on a green shimmer before his very eyes, bright and metallic. It was as if emeralds themselves were being used to paint the pages.

He became transfixed by this, deaf to the world around him. Like a thought being pushed violently to the front of his mind, however, he heard the very near sound of a latch being unlocked. Breath caught in his throat as he slammed the book closed and gathered up all of his papers. Felix's veins ran cold with panic. He didn't want Nonna Noxa to know he'd been snooping through her book. What could he do? Where was the squirrel? Where could he hide?

A quick glance to his left revealed an open cupboard. With a surprising level of stealth, Felix slid under a table, over a pile of bones, and into the small crevice with noiseless efficiency. To the boy's surprise, it wasn't the old wooden door that had unlocked, but the rusty hatch of the weathered clay stove. Its hinges let out a creaking moan as its door slowly slid open.

Though his lungs were straining for air, he repressed his breath to a silent wheeze. A dim line of light came into the cupboard through a slit in its hinges. He peered through and could see a thin hand with a drooping lace sleeve reach through the stove door. He wondered how anyone could have gotten themselves caught into such a tiny trap, though as the arm reached out, the opening stretched wider, like a yawning mouth.

Once the door had widened to the length of the wall, Nonna Noxa sauntered out of the opening, lace pure and white despite the soot around her. Though, what Felix noticed most was that the witch, for the first time since they'd met, had her veil pulled back. He'd never caught sight of her face before, and to be honest, the curiosity he'd had around it had since subsided. Though now as the boy peered through the crack in the cupboard, he couldn't peel his eyes away from her.

From what he could observe beyond their distance, she was improbably gaunt. Sweets seemed to have rotted each of her teeth down to nubs, though the rot didn't stop there. Her face was curdled into warts, and her bones had diminished to the point that she looked like a narrow spoon draped in skin. Her eyes captivated him the most. There was something not quite right about them, but he couldn't put his finger on what from where he sat. He stretched his neck to get a better look. As Felix strained, his foot reached to balance itself against what he thought was the edge of the cabinet. Though, as a quick clatter soon told him, it was not.

Nonna Noxa's slender head twisted towards the noise, her thin hair floating around her like wisps of silk. She drew nearer and nearer to the cupboard, a foul expression on her wrinkled mouth. Her hand reached out towards the cupboard door as Felix's breath became short and frantic. He could see her eyes as clear as day now. They were dark and yellow with wide pupils stretching from side to side. Staring into them was like staring into an abyss. Enchanting, endless, and hungry.

Her hand drew ever close, and Felix could see a wrath deepening along the lines of her face. Just before she grasped the cabinet knob, he heard a rustling from the shelves above him. Nonna Noxa's haunted eyes darted upward, and an annoyed scoff escaped her throat. "Vermin," she hissed. The witch reached out her hand and drew it back to her side. Felix could see the black squirrel clutched in her bony claw. "I've warned you rodents what would happen if you didn't leave this room be!"

The witch opened her mouth up wide, like a puppet, and Felix shuddered at what he saw within. Two tongues sat on the bottom of her jaw, one straining over the other as if it was fighting for dominance. With a twist, one of her tongues dislocated and the other squelched into place.

One speaks with reason, the other with rhyme, Felix thought to himself.

Nonna Noxa focused on the squirrel who wriggled in her hand. With the strike of a viper, the witch spat onto its face, and the squirrel recoiled with a chitter. She then spoke melodically in her bardic lilt:

> *"Black as the moon in great expanse,*
> *Yet silver sliver, given chance,*
> *Will part the morrow from its stance."*

A patch of white fur stained the tip of the squirrel's tail. To Felix's horror, his little companion began to writhe and contort in the witch's hand. Whiteness quickly spread with a hiss up the critter's body like a fuse, erasing the richness of its fur. It released a painful squeal. The final tuft of black over its nose was taken by white, and as it disappeared, a whisper of inky smoke hovered in the air like the final breath of a candle. The witch caught this in a small vial and placed it on the table.

She gripped her hand tighter around the white squirrel in her long fingers, and it instantly disintegrated into dust.

With this, she patted her hands clean and pulled her veil back over her face. Felix was frozen in abject terror. The boy ached to jump out and scream, but he couldn't. He knew he couldn't do much of anything while Nonna Noxa was still there. But her work appeared to be done anyway. The witch slowly began to glide away from the scene with her graceful, watery movements. He could hear a latch from the old door click as she left the room.

Once he knew it was clear, Felix crept from the cupboard. His fingertips grazed the dust that was once his sole remaining friend. The boy bit his lips to keep quiet, although he longed to cry aloud. As he stood, he came eye to eye with the vial of smoke the witch had placed onto the table. Its formlessness seemed as if it had taken the shape of the small squirrel, floating dreamily in the glass. With desperation, Felix gazed about the room. The stove was still open. Maybe there was a rare magic inside. Something that could fix this.

He quickly pocketed the small vial and carefully walked to the door of the stove with a feeling that he was entering into a hungry mouth. But what else could he do? So, armed with his optimistic finger, the boy entered the stove. He couldn't see much, for if the dim light of the last room was poor, then this one was downright impoverished. Only a weak orange glow lit the darkness as it sparked from the narrow walls, like embers embedded in the stone.

Though what the boy thought would be a small cavity in the wall was, in fact, much more. The embers trailed down, down, down into a dark tunnel. Felix carefully walked forward to find the first step along a set of stairs. He followed this deep into the earth below the manor. Thin branches lined the embered walls like vines bearing ripe plums. The deeper he ventured, the more plentiful the plums became.

A cool green light finally emitted from the tunnel. When he reached the source, he found a cavern filled with a small grove of plum trees. This sight was a cool wash of water for his struggling eyes. The smell that accompanied it, however, was less of a relief. A bitter, stinging scent like that of vinegar filled the cavern. Lanterns lined the walls, but they had been left extinguished. The only source of light now came from a series of short bottles sitting beside a chair that showed a looming algae-green glow.

Nonna Noxa's potions! Felix thought to himself. He'd watched her use them to perform great acts of magic. They would probably be able to heal the squirrel and then some! He rushed up to them in delight and held one in his hand. It was warm, as if it had just been cooked.

Felix was so excited that it took him several moments to notice a figure sitting in the chair behind him. His heart jumped, and with it, the rest of him. A yelp escaped his lips, but just as it did, he felt his bones grow cold. Sitting in the chair was the lifeless body of a boy, opened up like a jewelry box. It took a moment for him to process the victim's face among the dressings of blood and terror. Once it hit, though, it was clear that this had once been Curtis.

Felix fell down onto the hard, stony floor with a numb thud. He couldn't peel his eyes away from the horrified face of the dead boy he'd once called his friend. He noticed that at the very least the sickly green had been drained from Curtis's skin. Although, as Felix held the warm vial in his hand, he had a feeling he knew exactly where that green went.

In his delirium, he noticed Curtis's feet had an unusual shape to them as well. Among his many other desecrations, this seemed a small issue. As he stared longer, though, Felix saw that the feet were beginning to form roots. With a hoarse gasp, Felix darted his eyes around the cavern. He hadn't noticed before, but the trunks of each tree were all twisted into horrified human-like shapes. The shapes of children.

Felix felt sick. He wanted to vomit and cry and scream. His finger tingled. He didn't care. How could Nonna Noxa do this? If there was ever a time to be sad and bitter, it was now. His finger tingled again, harder this time. What did it expect Felix to do? He looked at the bottle in his hand. He wasn't sure what he could do, but maybe there was something he could try.

That night, the moon was nearly dark. Only a sliver of it still hung weakly in the sky. When everyone else was asleep, he slipped from his bed and went about the halls into a sitting room where he knew no one could hear him. The starlight shone through a nearby window, and Felix looked pleadingly onto its shimmer.

"Momma, Curtis, Scruff-Butt...wherever ya are," he paused and took in a deep breath, then continued, "wish me luck."

Felix took out the menacing bottle from the witch's cavern. Instantly, the starlit scene faded to a ghastly algae-green. He pulled off the cork and nearly gagged from its bitter scent. Carefully, Felix released three drops onto the black pane of the window and quickly replaced the cork. He looked into the shining reflection that the glass afforded.

Felix recalled a rhythm from Nonna Noxa's chants. He never remembered the words, but the beat with which she spoke always stuck with him. He clicked his tongue to the pace and twisted his fingers in tandem with the sound as if he too were weaving a tale.

The boy lifted his nubby fingernail over the pane and brought it down. After a few lackluster moments, Felix felt a shiver move down his spine, into the glass. Near instantly, he saw Nonna Noxa's image appear in the reflection: her thin white hair, emaciated skull, sideways eyes, and two vile tongues.

A tingle danced across his finger as he looked on the witch. He was scared and angry, but most of all, he was excited. A well of power surged up from his chest, through his throat, and into his mouth. He bent towards her grisly image and, against all better judgement, kissed it.

The power he felt dissipated. He hid away the glowing vial and looked upon the vision. The face of the wart-pocked witch had faded once again into starlight. Felix wasn't sure if his spell had any success. He hadn't followed it precisely as Nonna Noxa had taught it, but what he'd made do with felt right.

The next night was the dark moon, and the circle moved to convene. As the children were getting changed into their gray dress clothes, Felix escaped into the quiet sitting room. He pulled a linen handkerchief from his pocket and unfolded it to lay flat upon the floor. The boy took in a breath as he uncorked the green bottle. He allowed a single drop to fall upon the cloth before quickly resealing the cork.

Felix concentrated on the handkerchief, moving back and forward with the rhythm of his clicking tongue. It was more difficult to concentrate during the day, as he was nervous that someone would walk in on him. Eventually, though, the boy felt his mind spread away like a drop of water fallen into a pond.

He knew the magic had taken hold when the handkerchief began to throb before him like a living heart. With haste, Felix folded the handkerchief and placed it back into his pocket. His timing couldn't have been better, as not a moment later, the children began to march up the stairs towards their meeting place. Hurriedly, he scampered along behind them.

The group met in a room with a long table that stretched from end to end. Upon the table sat plates set for each child, a steaming cut of steak on each. The children had not eaten a bite all day, as instructed by Nonna Noxa, and by the time they arrived at the room, every one of them was ravenous. Those who had grown green with foul tempers were already primed to sink their teeth into something.

Felix, however, was far from hungry. When he laid eyes on the lace-draped witch standing calmly in the corner of the room, his stomach began to turn. She greeted all the children cheerily, gesturing them to their seats as they entered the room. It took painstaking effort for Felix to muster a smile for the wicked hag, but he managed nonetheless.

The boy looked down at the steak on his plate. It glistened with the syrups of well-cooked meat, and a vibrant red sparkled from its center like freshly polished rubies. The children's mouths were watering at this feast, but not Felix's. His mouth sat in a downturned line. All he thought of when he looked at the pound of flesh was Curtis, whose fate had been no luckier than this poor cow's.

"Welcome to your most valuable lesson of all, my plums," Nonna Noxa began. "Tonight, I will bestow great magic onto you. Magic which I would not entrust to just anyone. Are you all ready for this gift?"

Felix gazed around the lengthy table at the children. Many were beginning to show the same tinge of green in their skin that Curtis and Genevieve had. They nodded along to Nonna Noxa's questions, though they were slow and lethargic, like bloated dinner guests who couldn't refuse another bite.

"And you, sweet one?" Felix flinched as the witch's voice came over his shoulder. He turned to see her looming right behind him.

Felix gulped sharply and composed himself. "Yes'm. I'm ready."

Though her veil was thick, the boy could swear he saw the witch's long, black teeth creep out through a wide smile. "Wonderful. Now, this mighty spell is beholden to the whims of justice. It will work to ensnare those who dare face against you into a trap of their own making. It is the art of a true witch. Let us begin."

With this, Nonna Noxa reached into her long sleeve and pulled out that rancid green vial. She walked to each child's placement, and with a press of the switch, she released a drop of her wicked venom onto their steaks. Once she returned to the head of the table, the witch replaced the vial into her sleeve.

Felix knew he had to act quick. He reached into his pocket and felt the pulsating handkerchief. His fingers rummaged about a bit more, uncovering a small iron nail. The very same sort of nail that had been causing him so much anguish these many days. With sleight, he snuck a precise kiss onto the tip of the nail and slipped it back into his pocket without anyone seeing him do so.

The boy then strained his ears to concentrate tenderly on the witch. She extended her arms to begin weaving her tale, and as she did, the faintest whisper of a squelch slid from behind her veil. Right at the sound of her second tongue, Felix plunged the iron into his handkerchief. Did it work? The witch made no reaction, but he hoped dearly that he wasn't about to walk into his own demise. Not a moment later, did the witch begin her bitter verse:

"It buzzes, it whizzes, it was with a flare,
The morsel, the missile, the mite in the air.
Mrs. Toad, she forebode, the filigree fly,
From the frond in her pond where the snack drifted by.
Though flimsy, with whimsy, took lap after lap,
Yet bumbled a stumble into Mrs. Toad's trap.
As it blundered, she wondered, her heart all a-flutter.
Should she dine with some wine and a bitty of butter?
But nary so merry Mrs. Toad, she did feel,
So with chomp and not pomp she made it her—"

"Wheel!" Felix blurted.

Nonna Noxa's weaving tale abruptly came to a halt as if the earth itself had ceased to move beneath her. The children all turned their heads towards Felix with sneers of annoyed confusion; why, after all, would he interrupt the witch's spell?

With an impatient chortle, Nonna Noxa said, "please holster your zeal." She attempted then to get her story back on track, but Felix was quick behind her.

"But I'm bored of your spiel."

A gasp slipped from the lips of a few children; a twinge of anger shivered across Nonna Noxa's lace.

"My dear, what's brought this appeal?"

"Just that I know you're a slippery eel. And that you can't peel your tongue from its seal."

A sly smirk lifted across Felix's face as he watched the witch stand silently for a moment. He could feel the handkerchief begin to struggle in his pocket as she attempted to free her reasoning tongue from his spell. She reached up behind her veil and frantically pried at her jaw, but the iron nail held steadfast. The children were beginning to murmur in confusion. At this, Nonna Noxa dropped her hands to her side and regained her composure.

"Well, let's make a deal."

"You think that will heal? All the children you steal and make into your meal?"

Nonna Noxa began to slowly move from the head of the table towards Felix, but he quickly leapt from his seat. He dashed to the other end of the table, nimbly avoiding the witch.

"If I could repeal..."

"Then your lies become real, and it would conceal."

"That...would be ideal."

Nonna Noxa was now lunging for Felix, violently shoving children out of the way and leaning over the table to grab at him. The boy was too quick for her, though, both with his feet and with his tongue. He was amazed at how easily the mirroring spell allowed Nonna Noxa's rhymes to come to him.

"But I will reveal this evil ordeal. You make us bitter until we congeal up from our head and down to our heel."

"Your claims are surreal!"

"Then as we squeal, you cut us with steel to drain us of poisons vert, lime, and teal."

Nonna Noxa's great age began to show as her watery grace faltered. The witch's steps became lumbered, and her pure white lace was now stained with the ochre oils of meat. Nonna Noxa lunged again at Felix, but he jumped onto the tabletop, towering above the old witch.

"You...you..." the witch stammered over herself, anger and frustration choking her voice.

The children had gotten up from their seats and were backing away from her. Those with a green tinge in their skin were now examining themselves as if they were seeing the hue for the first time. Nonna Noxa's great laced head whipped from one direction to another as she watched her carefully woven web of secrets begin to unravel.

"Stop..." she began, "cease this at once, you...you beetle!" But just as she said this, she instantly recoiled in regret. Her hands clapped to her mouth as if trying to pull the words back in, but it was too late.

Felix took a step towards the witch, looking down at her like she was a little mouse. "That doesn't rhyme, Nonna Noxa...so *kneel*." He smiled widely with a victorious twinkle in his eye.

The old witch began to whimper, then gag and cough. A hissing sound streamed out of her mouth as ash fell from behind her veil. Enough ash, one might think, to make up the mass of a tongue. Slowly, she crumpled to the floor, her arms and legs curling in on themselves. Black spots of soot began to blossom across the white of her lace, and the very walls of the old manor shook as her magic was undone, one delicate spell after another.

A crack sounded from Felix's jacket pocket, and a shadow spiraled out onto the boy's shoulder. Felix's heart leapt as the shadow gained weight and soon took the shape of a familiar black squirrel. It stared down coldly at the withering witch, who was now just a disheveled clump of dusty lace bunched up on the floor. The children watched the material warily, moving in with growing suspicion. Felix hopped off the table and approached her with the rest. Nonna Noxa was so thin now, almost flat. With a deep breath, Felix reached down to lift her veil as all of the children watched on.

A wrinkled coat of skin sat beneath her lace, looking back up at them. Gasps circled around the group as they jolted back. But Felix leaned in closer. He saw skin but nothing else. No slender bones, no black teeth, and no haunting eyes. He reached down to pull at her and the skin lifted easily from the heap like the casing of a sausage.

What happened to the rest of the witch, the children never knew. That night, however, was the last night many of them saw each other again. They warmed themselves by the hearth kindled by lace and shed skin. The green children hadn't faded back to their original colors, nor had their moods softened much. It seemed Nonna Noxa's magic hadn't caused that. Maybe they would be able to heal themselves. Or maybe it was just something they would have to learn to live with, a bitter memory rotting beneath their skin.

When Felix awoke the next morning, a bittersweet weight seemed to drape his mind. He didn't want to leave behind the hope that he'd once sought from the manor, but he looked forward to what new hope he might find. Now, with his squirrel companion on his shoulder, the boy took his first step from the manor's walls.

Grasses and flowers now surrounded the once dead swamp, and the briars themselves seemed to pulse with youth. Felix wasn't sure how long he'd been in the witch's web, or what waited for him now that he left, but he knew that home was the only place he wanted to be. Lord willing of course, he hoped that Momma would be inclined to find some room in her home for squirrels. With Felix's newfound talents, though, he was sure he could help them make do.

Black squirrels still roam Allium and find their ways into towns. They say that seeing one is a sign that magic is near. But be careful if it leads you into the swamps, for you might just meet the witch of the briars who wants nothing more than the bitter poisons of a once sweet heart to fuel her wicked spells. If anything, just remember to beware what lurks behind white lace.

Wayward Lines

The witch who's true holds twice the blood of
mortal kind.

One red and warm, as what in any man will find.

The other is a blood, less easy understood by such a plan.

It beats its way not through the veins, but yet somehow
it can,

Mark a kindred lineage through time and generation.

So, do these bonds defy the rules of birth and blood
and nation.

As magic lives where stable truth
begins to take its leave,

The source of
such a talent is
wayward
from its eve.

Then from
that seed
it stems its
way through
branches of
this tree,

To form
a line of
relatives with
magic in
their pedigree.

Chapter Nine

A Ledger of Wonders

Here are transcribed several accounts of witchery from folks of all kinds across the region. Within these ledgers are discoveries found by many who have seen the magical works enacted by a conjuring witch. Each of these details shows a unique form of magic that has been used to help or hinder the wary folk, as well as the means by which they came upon this magic in the first place.

If you choose to follow along with any of these workings, know that not every spell need be followed to the letter. These witches worked with what their land provided, and so may you. Remember, however—as these witches too well know—good work shows good results, substitutions must be made with necessity over convenience, and one without wonder ends only in blunder.

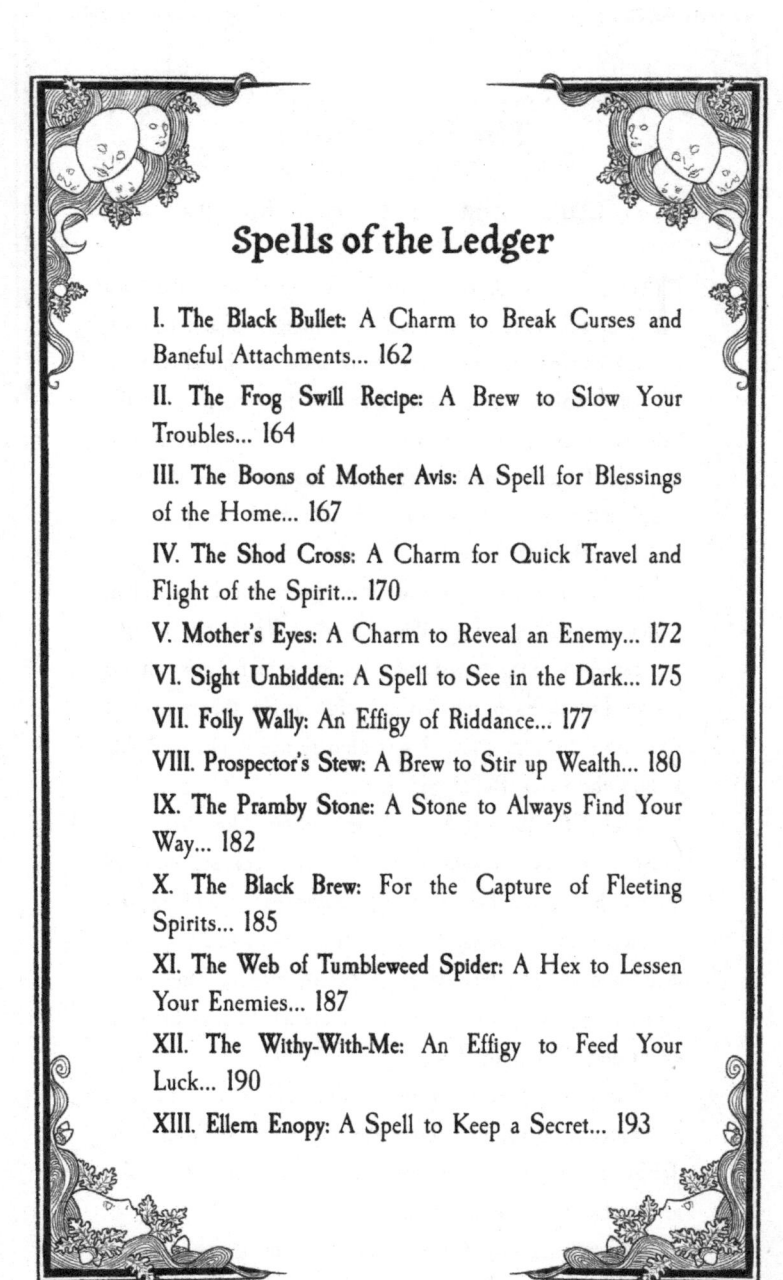

Spells of the Ledger

I. The Black Bullet: A Charm to Break Curses and Baneful Attachments... 162

II. The Frog Swill Recipe: A Brew to Slow Your Troubles... 164

III. The Boons of Mother Avis: A Spell for Blessings of the Home... 167

IV. The Shod Cross: A Charm for Quick Travel and Flight of the Spirit... 170

V. Mother's Eyes: A Charm to Reveal an Enemy... 172

VI. Sight Unbidden: A Spell to See in the Dark... 175

VII. Folly Wally: An Effigy of Riddance... 177

VIII. Prospector's Stew: A Brew to Stir up Wealth... 180

IX. The Pramby Stone: A Stone to Always Find Your Way... 182

X. The Black Brew: For the Capture of Fleeting Spirits... 185

XI. The Web of Tumbleweed Spider: A Hex to Lessen Your Enemies... 187

XII. The Withy-With-Me: An Effigy to Feed Your Luck... 190

XIII. Ellem Enopy: A Spell to Keep a Secret... 193

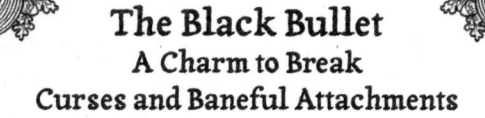

The Black Bullet
A Charm to Break
Curses and Baneful Attachments

There is a witch that goes by Tabby Boots. She lives near the bend of the river in a humble shack beneath an old catalpa tree with leaves as wide as shovel spades. Ill-wished folks would gather from all four corners of the valley to partake in her treatments, but one most of all had become the most sought after. This was the Black Bullet, a small pellet charm constructed for the absolution of curses and unearthly attachments.

She'd once taken me into her shack, for I had fallen under the workings of a malevolent spirit. The witch thought me asleep as she awayed into her stregareum, her witch's room. But through the tattered old curtain that separated this room from the rest, I was able to see it all. And this is how the Black Bullet was made.

Tabby Boots pulled a cupped stone, like that of a mortar, onto a slab and gathered several jars and pouches around her. I saw her reach into these vessels and pull all manner of foul material. Some of it appeared to be salt and dried worms. The rest simply appeared withered and dead. Curious as I was, I'd assume the material differed for each client and their rightful woes.

She ground these each to a powder. The witch then took a weathered fat candle, whose wax was black as lamp soot. Tabby Boots poured this wax over the powder until it was as flooded as it was powdered.

The witch scooped the mixture into her knobby hands and began to roll it all into a ball, near the size of a cat's eye, as she sang:

"Widow Tallow, mourning still,
Your veil prevails the woeful will.
Mourn for the wicked and mourn for the plight,
Mourn for the worm who's seen its last night.
Iron shell and black shot shoe,
The Widow Tallow takes her due."

The next I'd known, Tabby Boots had come from her stregareum and neared to loom over my wretched shape. As I feigned slumber, she dug her bony finger into my mouth, to which my eyes opened wide against my behest. She withdrew her digit and slathered my expectorant over the waxen ball.

The witch then ushered me up to stand, though I could feel the wicked spirit trying to drag me back down. She took a kind of iron plate, something akin to part of an old gate hinge or maybe a small trivet. I'm not sure its constructed purpose had as much relevance here as did its material. She placed the plate over the ball and helped me to position my foot on top of it.

With all the force I had left in me, she told me to stomp down onto the plate and crush the Black Bullet underneath. I was weak, so it took great effort, but I did it sure enough. Just as I felt the bullet crumble beneath my step, my wits returned to me as if a fever had broken away in an instant. It was then that I knew the spirit was gone.

Tabby Boots can still be found out by the river bend, beneath the old catalpa, dealing her Black Bullets to the wretched and maledicted, like I'd once been. I myself haven't been to see her again. But should the need arise, I know now what to do.

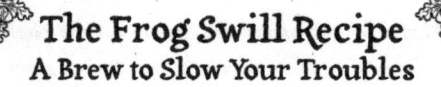

The Frog Swill Recipe
A Brew to Slow Your Troubles

There is a place that we call "Menace Stump" deep in the woods. It's where an ancient tree died and fell of its own accord, leaving a hollow bowl of lumber in its place. When it rains, the stump fills up, and hordes of frogs and toads congregate to catch flies and make merry the way that frogs do. Some say they can hear whispered voices among the croaks. Rumors spread that the stump is haunted by the ghosts of children who were lost in the woods, or that witches gather there to sing, dance, and drink with the frogs.

One day, when I was young, I was chased by some bullies after school, and I managed to lose them when I took a turn into the woods. It wasn't long before I came upon Menace Stump, well-quenched and splayed before me. I knew the old rumors were just stories; yet there was a depth to the stump that I couldn't explain. I turned to leave, but a boy appeared before me. He was just slightly younger than I was at the time, with wild hair and a scruffy, striped coat.

The boy had an aura about him, something I couldn't quite place. With the twinge of a mischievous grin, he told me he could stop my bullies. All I would need to do was return one night when the town was asleep and bring with me a potato, a bowl, a pot, and four stones gathered from a grave. I was suspicious but desperate and did not question the boy.

That night, I returned to Menace Stump where I found him kindling a fire. As I neared, I could see that he was throwing tufts of hair into the flames, short and soft like that of a rabbit. I gave him the items he asked for, and the boy quickly set to work.

He took the bowl and filled it with water from the hollow of the stump. The boy then pulled a knife from his pocket to peel and cut the potato. This he tossed into the water, churning the lot until the water turned pale with starch. He then poured the water—save for the potatoes—into the pot and nestled this over the fire.

Next, he told me to throw the four gravestones into the pot. After that, the boy pulled a leather lace from his other pocket and handed it over to me. I was instructed to tie one knot into the lace for each of my enemies, naming them as the bind was made. Once I'd done this, he took the lace from me and tossed it into the pot. He lifted a long stick and began to stir the waters, chanting to himself:

> *"Quick as the spark, the tongue is quicker,*
> *Lickety split and thicker, thicker!*
> *Still as death and waif as wicker,*
> *Swell the swill and thicker, thicker!"*

The boy continued to chant this until the waters became thick like syrup. Lifting his stick, the knotted lace was pulled from the water, which he motioned towards me. The boy said that when next I saw my bullies, I had to throw this at their feet to make them stop. He told me, though, that if I'd tied pieces of their likeness such as hair or fingernails into the knots, or used their shoelaces rather than the leather lace, I wouldn't need to throw the knots at their feet to make it work.

Well, the day after this odd encounter, I did see my bullies. They sought me out again after school, but I was ready for them this time. I threw the lace at their feet, and at first, nothing happened. But soon enough, they began to slow. A moment after, they stopped all together, standing around like lost children.

I ran, but they never caught up to me. Ever. I would see them from time to time, and whenever I did, they seemed to slow down again. It was like they were swimming through syrup, drowsy and confused. I wanted to return to Menace Stump to thank the boy, but he never showed himself to me again. Still, in the dead of night, after rain had filled the stump and frogs returned to sing their praises, I would collect a little more water for myself. To this day, the mysterious Frog Swill recipe still works to slow my troubles.

The Boons
of Mother Avis
A Spell for Blessings of the Home

One late night, when the skies were as black as bramble berries, I came walking back down the old dirt road from a long day's work. I heard a voice lilting in the darkness and looked around to see its source. There was an old brown plot beside the hedge stones that had sat vacant and barren for as long as I'd known. No one even set foot there, saying the dirt was sick and would turn the onlooker rancid too.

But that night, I saw the figure of a young woman in the darkness with a bright lantern by her side. I took cover by the stones to hide myself and steal a closer look. She stood in the plot, preparing something, it seemed. The woman kneeled down beside the lantern with what appeared to be a well-preserved bird's nest in her hand.

She reached into a satchel by her side and plucked out two jars of spices. She sprinkled these over the nest and into the lantern fire. I'd recognize the smells of cinnamon and cumin seed anywhere. They were my mother's favorite cooking spices, and they always smelled like home to me.

The woman stood back up with the nest in hand and began to walk along a set of lines that she had traced in the dirt before I arrived. As she did so, she sang to herself a funny song:

> *"Oh, Mother Avis, spin your nest,*
> *Spin with the strand that holds its best.*
> *Chick, chickadee, chick-a-delight,*
> *Twiddle, twitter, tweet all day and night.*
> *By mother's work, it takes its form,*

With mother's love, she keeps it warm.
Chick, chickadee, chick-a-delight,
Twiddle, twitter, tweet all day and night.
Fruit, fettle, seed into her dome,
All that she chooses makes a home.
Chick, chickadee, chick-a-delight,
Twiddle, twitter, tweet all day and night."

She made this walk four times as she sang her song, then returned to the lantern in the center. The woman began to pull items from her satchel—bric-a-brac, it seemed to me. For each one, she declared something and set it into the nest.

"Wealth," she said for a coin. "Growth," she said for a pumpkin seed. "Beauty," she said for a lovely broach. "Luxury," she said for a small silver spoon. And "secrets," she said for a key-less lock. The woman then blew out her lantern, and all was dark.

The next day, I had nearly forgotten about the oddity I happened upon the night before. On my way to work, I passed the brown lot, as usual, but to my shock, it was no longer brown. Green buds and flowers had begun to sprout overnight. I thought about the woman and began wondering if she somehow caused this.

A few days later, construction had begun on the plot, framing a house oddly the same size as the lines the woman traced. Even stranger, this home was finished not even a week later. And it was truly beautiful, with ornate banisters, stained glass windows, and gabled roofs. The land itself was abundant with growth. Fields around it were bursting with crops. And who came out from the home, as if she'd lived there in luxury for years, but the young woman I saw that one dark night.

It was unbelievable. Everything she placed into the nest had come into being. Wealth, growth, beauty, and luxury. But it left me wondering with a hapless pit in my stomach. Why had she placed "secrets" into the nest as well?

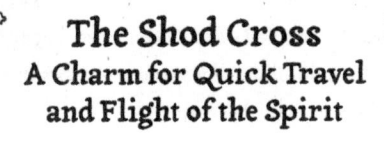

The Shod Cross
A Charm for Quick Travel
and Flight of the Spirit

My Grampa told me once that every time thunder rolled over his home, he would catch sight of a dark woman riding between lightning strikes on a penny-colored horse. She would flit across the prairies, over houses, and under porches as if she were grass on the wind.

One day, when the thunder rumbled, he met the woman and saw how tired and feeble the horse had become. Dotingly, he offered her a trade. He would make her the warmest, sturdiest pair of boots that she ever saw if he could have her horse for one day. She accepted, and when the lightning struck again, she was gone. But her penny horse still stood beside my Grampa.

Now, he didn't actually ride the horse at all. Instead, he brought it into his work shed and dried it off. He fed the horse a bucket of oats and let it drink from his fresh spring. Grampa even shod the horse, replacing its old rusty shoes and nails for fresh new ones.

When the woman returned, she took the horse's reins and pulled it back into the storm. Mounting the horse, she coaxed it forward, but it would not fly. Angry, the woman whipped and kicked the horse. Finally, she looked down at its hooves suddenly becoming furious to see it wearing new shoes. She moved to dismount and rage towards at Grampa, but the horse bucked, throwing her off. She landed hard with a crash of thunder, and the two were gone.

A few days later, my Grampa found the horseshoe nails still sitting on his bench. And so, to remember the experience, he made a charm out of them. One nail to travel east and west, one nail to travel north and south, and one nail to travel high and low. Using copper wire, he bound these together on a stormy day in the shape of a six-armed cross.

He said that whenever he wore this cross, his cart would ride faster, his pace was quicker, and even the roads were clearer. Not only that, but in his dreams, he would find himself traveling all across the prairies like he'd seen the woman do when thunder rolled.

He had a method, he told me, that in waking hours he would sway the cross in front of him, forward and back, and he would sway with it. When he felt himself fall into a waking sleep, he would stop moving but allow the cross to continue. He said that it felt like while his body stilled, his ghost didn't, and it would slip right out of his bones.

Now, Grampa eventually lost those nails to memory. He was saddened to see them go. But then it seemed that a similar cross made by any trio of worn horseshoe nails would hold the same power. He believed that in thanks for what kindness it was shown on that one stormy day, the spirit of the penny horse was still with him. And each time the charm was made, it retained the notion to fly.

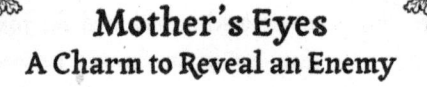

Mother's Eyes
A Charm to Reveal an Enemy

There was a cottage at the edge of town. It was lovely, like a fairy tale, with a garden that seemed to bloom well through the winter and bear fruit even in the spring. But even as it was, we all avoided it as if it were death itself. An odd man lived there. His dress and manner were quite unusual, and his gaze could pierce through brick walls, closed doors, and some would say, even our souls themselves.

But I was desperate, and if anyone could help me, it was him. I'd found myself in a bit of a predicament as of late. Gossip had begun to spread on my name, and sabotage had fallen in my path at every turn. So, there I was, at the unseasonal cottage of Mickle McCoy. He let me in, sat me down with a cup of hot cider—as if he'd already expected me—and gazed into my soul as he was known to do.

He told me that, to solve my problem, I must go into his garden and find the motherwort that grew along the east patch's edge. It was a tall herb with a thick square stem and leaves like a grandmother's hands. This, he said, was a strong protective guardian with the abilities to know. I did not yet understand what he meant by this, but he went on.

Mickle told me to take the tallest stalk in the patch which bears the prickles on its crown. I was to strip it of its foliage until all that remained was the stalk itself. I must then cut it at its segments into four even rods. The unusual man told me I must, too, find a black walnut's shell that had been holed by a squirrel's bite and twine the color of my mother's eyes, which watch over me even in my absence.

I told him, "My mother has never been one to lend her watchfulness to my aid."

"Then you take it from her by force," he said to me in a casual tone.

He then continued to explain that I would need to bind the stalks together with the twine to create a diamond. Then I must string the twine from corner to corner to make a cross and thread the shell through the cross's center.

I did so, and once the charm was constructed, I returned to him. The man took this contraption in his hands and touched it to my brow, touched it to my lips, touched it to my heart, and touched it to the shadow beneath my feet. He then instructed me to gaze through the hole of the shell with my right eye and turn to face all four directions around me as he spoke:

> *"Four corners in four corners lie,*
> *Where none escapes the mother's eye.*
> *She knows what's done, she hears what's said,*
> *She has eyes behind her head.*
> *Mother's eyes will strip you bare,*
> *To know your truth within her care."*

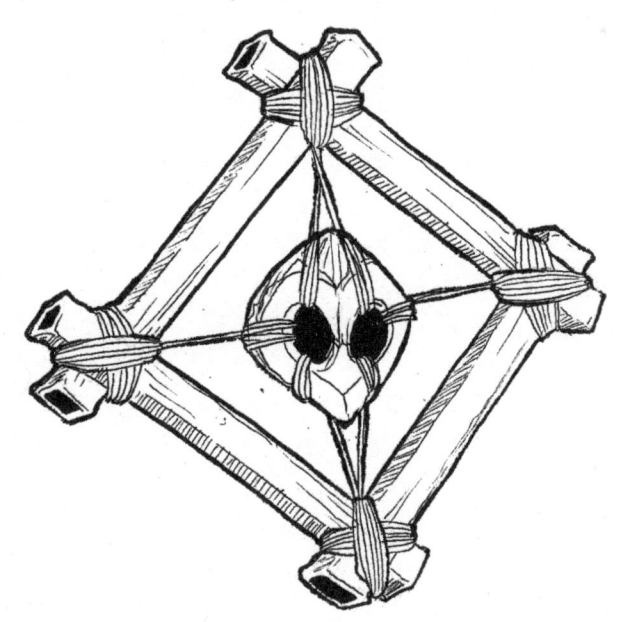

He told me then to keep the charm in my pocket, wear it about my neck, or hang it above my door. Those who were traitors among me would soon make themselves known. Sure enough, just as he said, some whom I considered friends proved themselves much less. When confronted, they could barely thread a lie together to save themselves, or at times were instantly overwhelmed with confession.

As long as I keep the eye in its place, I've noticed that any who mean me cruel intent are soon revealed in one way or another. Luckily for me, these people are few and far between. And those who are revealed as wicked rarely garner trust from anyone else. Maybe once they've proven themselves more noble, the eye will turn its gaze from them. But until then, I will not fret to see them suffer.

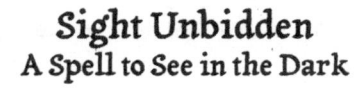

Sight Unbidden
A Spell to See in the Dark

The night was never one too kind to us country folk. It is a black wall that keeps us held tight in place until the sun chases it away. When it appears, we must heed its warnings in genuflect until such a time it decides we may stir again. Only the unbidden may move about in the night's mantle. This was something that my family and I knew all too well. We had no business knowing about what things moved around under darkness.

But one night, when the shadows came and my parents and cousins went to bed, I heard a rustling on the stairs. It was unusual for anyone to still be moving around at this hour. I was sure it must be another squirrel that had gotten in through the broken windowpane. I slid from my bed quietly, hoping to usher it away without waking up the others before it could get to the grains.

But at the foot of the stairs, in what little light the dying embers of our hearth afforded, I saw my sister standing by the door in a black cloak. I was going to sass her for scaring me so late in the night, but my curiosity got to me first when I saw her pull a small black pouch from a lace around her neck.

She went to the fire and pulled out two black coals, which had long since cooled. These she dropped into her pouch along with a yellow bloom, which I recognized to be an evening primrose, whose flower most often wakes when the rest of us retire. My sister tightened the pouch closed and placed it around her neck again, muttering to herself:

> *"Eyes like coal in shadow's shroud,*
> *Blinded by the darkest cloud.*
> *I take the night now into me,*
> *With blackest sight to let me see."*

With that, my sister swept through the house like a cat and out the door. I couldn't believe it. Had my sister become one of the unbidden? I needed to find out. And so, I took a black sock and placed two coals inside with an evening primrose flower that bloomed outside our window. I tied this around my neck and mirrored the words I heard my sister say.

As if they were now taking their first breaths, my eyes widened in the darkness. What was black now became a blue-like haze of foggy light, and every corner emerged from hiding. It was beautiful. Outside, shadows danced with the starlight like wights in the wind. I was certain I could see the spirits of things like trees and rocks being worn about themselves like coats. The black wall of night had suddenly become a door.

I did not see my sister again until morning. She was her quiet, well-mannered self as always. As she folded laundry from the line, I wondered how many other things she knew as one of the unbidden. When had she turned? How had she turned? And how could I become one of the unbidden as well?

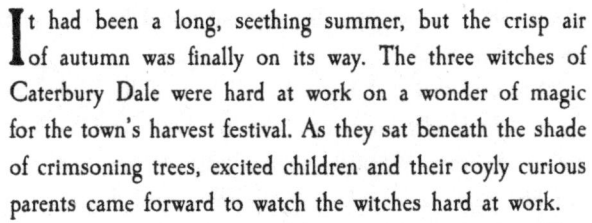

Folly Wally
An Effigy of Riddance

It had been a long, seething summer, but the crisp air of autumn was finally on its way. The three witches of Caterbury Dale were hard at work on a wonder of magic for the town's harvest festival. As they sat beneath the shade of crimsoning trees, excited children and their coyly curious parents came forward to watch the witches hard at work.

Roxanne, dressed all in white, was often the friendliest of the bunch. At her side was a basket of yarn, feathers, and other curios which she'd been sorting into tidy little piles. With a shy smile, Roxanne began to tell us a story. She recounted a time when the three of them had wandered into the woods on an early autumn day. There they met a creature shaped only of bones.

Peculiar as he was, they weren't afraid, but instead rather curious. They asked him who he was, but he didn't have much to tell. The creature said his bones were of those left in the forest and then forgotten. Now he was empty and bare without name or tale to tell. Well, as little girls often did, Roxanne and her friends had many tales to tell. And so, the three talked to him about their woes, as small and trifle as they might have seemed.

The girls noted that the creature seemed quite cold. With every breeze, his bones would rattle and teeth would chatter. So, as the girls spoke, they took out some yarn and needles then began to knit. Once they were done—with their knitting and tales alike—they offered their wares to him, and they instantly felt their worries leave them as well. Not only that, but all the things which they had complained to him seemed to resolve themselves soon after.

Maxine, the liveliest of the three, dressed all in red, nodded fiercely along with Roxanne's tale. She'd been binding together thin reeds into the crude shape of a man. The red witch told us how they had not seen the creature again, but they knew he was still out there. Why? Ever since, the three had continued to knit and speak their woe into their yarn. They would then leave what they made by the woods. The next day, the garment would be gone, and so too their troubles.

She said that they began to call him "Folly Wally," as he was the kindly bone man who was kept warm by their follies and woes. When the weather began to cool and their troubles began to rise, his kinship was needed the most.

Vixenne, dressed all in black and truly the wisest of the three, spoke up. She had been sewing acorns into a quilted swatch as the other two explained. She spoke of how they began to build an effigy in Folly Wally's honor every autumn to continue their tradition. Before they dutifully collected their fresh acorns for the year by the fifteenth of September, they gathered all the old, unused ones that had not been employed in their spells.

These Vixenne sewed into a swatch of cloth cut from old clothes, dressing buttons and quilting a face onto what would represent Folly Wally's head. All the while, Maxine fashioned a body of sticks on which to fasten the head, and sweet Roxanne gathered yarn, feathers, beads, and strips of cloth to make his clothing.

Whenever one of them ran into trouble, they simply took an item for his dressings and tied it to the effigy's body while reciting a quaint little rhyme:

"Folly Wally, Folly Wally,
'Fore the land bears naught but Holly.
Take my woes unto your form,
And take these wares to keep you warm."

Little by little, the witches—and now the townsfolk as well—would leave their sorrows behind to keep Folly Wally warm as the weather got colder. At the winter solstice, Roxanne, Maxine, and Vixenne would take the fully dressed effigy to the woods. And well enough the witches of Caterbury Dale knew that Folly Wally was still out there, as their troubles would always wither away.

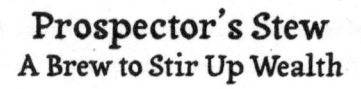

Prospector's Stew
A Brew to Stir Up Wealth

Old Jim Billy was a funny man. It's said he once worked at the mines, pickin' coal. 'Course, he soon ended up cookin' stew for us late-nighters down at the railroad station. He kicked up a dang nice stew, but most folks thought he'd done filled his skull with too much soot an' left himself fog-headed. Jim Billy often told us to enjoy his cookin' as long as we could, 'cause pretty soon he'd strike it rich, an' we wouldn't see no more of him after that.

Me an' the other fellas would just laugh him off, but one night, I saw him gatherin' up some water from the lake at high tide into a copper pot. I'm no cook, an' I know squat about good flavorin', but I do know what they been dumpin' in that lake, an' I hoped to hope that he wasn't usin' it to make our stew. But he just left the pot hooded on the stove overnight. The next mornin', though, after a storm had washed away a nearly full moon, I saw him collectin' rainwater into the pot as well. One mornin' later, I saw him again, this time by the field hedges, gatherin' dew drops from a stalk of goldenrod into a small flask. Sure enough, the dew water also got stirred into the pot with the rest.

What was the old coot up to? Curious, I followed him an' peaked my eye through a knot hole in one of the kitchen wall boards. I saw as he tossed a chunk of fool's gold an' a gypsum stone into the pot. He stirred the waters with his old wooden spoon—one which he'd used to feed dozens of us guys and more—an' sang with it a little song:

> "A mickle in and a penny out,
> A penny in my purse, no doubt!
> Copper, copper, bubble and bake,
> A penny will a dollar make."

He then took a penny from his pocket an' tossed this into the spinnin' waters. He said to the water, this time in an almost reprimandin' tone:

"Keep this gold, I am no fool,
Nor a ghost to spend these jewels,
But rich I'll be from coppered gruel."

Well, from there, Jim Billy hooded his pot once more. I scrambled away as he then walked out. Every night after, though, I saw him retire to the kitchen once supper ended. I would watch him drop another penny into the pot an' reprimand the pot with those same three lines.

Each night, I noticed that the gypsum stone became smaller an' smaller. Finally, when it was completely gone, a giddy smirk stretched across his near toothless mouth. He gathered up pennies from the slurry into his pockets, then hefted the pot into his arms. He poked his head through the door to see if any stragglers were still hangin' around the mess hall. Luckily, I'd tucked myself away behind a coal bin when I saw him comin'.

From there, the coot waddled out back to a tree that stood there, startin' to sprout some kind of fruit; I didn't know which kind. He poured the slurry out over its roots. The smile cracked out even wider over his face as he trotted his way back to the mess hall. I even saw him kick his heels together once or twice.

A handful of weeks passed, and his mood only got more shine to it. First, his scrappy shoes were replaced with a dapper new pair. Then the gaps in his gums were filled with gleaming gold teeth. Eventually, I stopped seein' him at the railroad at all. But every now an' then, he'd open the doors to his new mansion out in the city for us railroad boys, an' we'd all sit down for supper together again. These days, I always volunteer to clean the pots, with a few pennies in my pockets just in case.

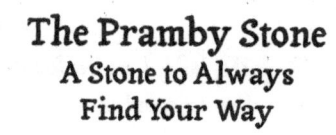

The Pramby Stone
A Stone to Always
Find Your Way

I'm no witch. I can't cast no spells, see no spirits, or know what hasn't yet come to pass. But I do have a bit of magic. The "Pramby Stone" is what my ma called it. It's small magic, but even small magic used right can change the course of a life. The stone's enchanted in that it only rolls towards what you seek. With it, I can find treasures, lost things, and my way through the dark. Ma said it can even help you find your fate.

She learned this work from her ma, and Gammy said she learned it from a gray woman she'd met by the lake. It was winter, as she tells it, coldest days of the year. She'd been dressed in woolen yarn from head to toe, but she could still feel the wind biting through every layer.

Against her better judgement, she cut through the shore to get home. The waters were colder than ice and hit harder than a wagon of rocks. The lake wouldn't think twice about eating you up at this time of year—always seemed like it was watching you as if it were a hungry panther behind a low hedge. 'Course, this was the quickest way back home, and night was coming soon. Gammy rolled the dice and decided the water was a safer bet than the dark.

She sped over the rocks that marked the shore to the lake. With the slick frost and crashing waves, she'd nearly slipped in more than once. Luckily, she'd caught herself on the stones, though the sharp edges did cut her hands up some and she'd seen a few drops of blood get gobbled up by the water. Somehow, she made it to the other end still in one piece. An old woman was standing there— "a hag," my Gammy used to describe her, though that term has tapered off since she's entered her silver era.

The woman was sallow-skinned and haggard. She wore a long gray dress, too thin for the cold. She stared at my Gammy, "eyes like a lynx," Gammy would say. She didn't know how, but she knew the woman was hungry, though her expression was still as ice. Gammy pulled a baked potato from her pocket, which she often held there to keep warm, and handed it to the woman. Her face broke into a sincere smile, though a red hue in the corners of her teeth did concern Gammy.

The gray crone said she'd been so hungry and waiting for someone to come by and offer her something to eat, but no one did. In thanks for the warm meal, she said she'd give Gammy something to always help find her way—as long as she promised to come by and feed her something warm when the days turn cold again.

Here's what the gray crone told Gammy to do: find for yourself a portion of dust from a crossroads. Take about a thumb tip to knuckle's worth of it and get it wet enough to ply like clay. Mix the clay with dried moss from the north side of a tree and barbs from the feather of a migrating bird. Mold this around a hungry lodestone, forming a ball somewhat the size of a cat's eye. The ball must then be left to dry until hard as stone by a fire that you yourself use for warmth and living. This is important, for if the ball is left to dry on its own or beside a fire that carries no bearing on your own life, it will hold no magic in turn.

Well, Gammy took the woman's words, and whether out of curiosity or boredom, she concocted the Pramby Stone to the gray crone's instructions. Funny enough, when she dropped the stone with a question in mind, or spun it on the floor like a top, wherever it rolled she found that what she sought was not far along. And so, the recipe for this work was passed down and down again, and now I pass it to you. Gammy still goes to the lake on cold winter days to feed the gray crone. Though, she has since learned that the crone does not care for potatoes.

The Black Brew
For the Capture
of Fleeting Spirits

It is well known that spirits move freely in our world whether we witness it or not. They dance and work, make merry and wary, all throughout the year. When wintertime comes, however, the spirits must prepare for their journeys. Frost makes poor fellows of the green folk and so, they will often retreat to the specter lands while the dark-time guard comes in to keep watch.

But before the spirits pass on, they'll often make their winter's gambit to take their leave. The door to the other side is narrow, of course, and the spirits must be quite slight to make their way through. To do this, they will shed their spirit skins, which contain the hefts of magic that they've built up over the sunny days. Folks around here call these sheddings "the Twixtlings."

It's the leaves, ripening fruits, and nuts that hold this magic. When they split off and flutter to the ground is when you know that a Twixtling has been released. The spirits have no use for this magic, you know. In the specter lands, keeping magic is like carrying water on the river. And so, this magic is usually just sent back into the soil, to melt with the return of spring.

But if you can catch a Twixtling before it touches the ground, then you just may have a proper chance at keeping that magic for yourself. Used wisely, you can send it on to many wonderful tasks. You may use it to call the dead back to speak to you or to journey into the specter lands themselves. I've known some to even use Twixtlings for retrieving things lost to them, be they memories, treasures, senses, or wits. Now there are well enough ways of doing this, but us witches around here have a fine method all our own.

A Witch's Book of Terribles

First, we fill a pot with local waters from the shores or banks of the land. The lake is where I gather mine, and if collected during a waning moon, it will be all the more potent. Simmer this over a yellow flame, and as it simmers, stir in hibiscus petals and madder root. When the pot begins to bleed, say:

> *"Like blood, like blood, like a running horse,*
> *Let life like luck refine its course."*

Stir in half a ladle's worth of quicklime and wait for the brew to darken. Once this is done, we'll contribute a baby's tooth, a day lily's blossom, the shell of a robin's egg, and a palmful of oak galls. This we'll keep a close eye over, waiting for it to blacken. When it is like ink, scatter in two spoons of vinegar. As the potion froths, the witches croon their song:

> *"By breath, by wisp of fleeting sorrow,*
> *Black before the dawn of morrow.*
> *Here within this midnight's broth,*
> *Catch the hedge veil's thinning cloth.*
> *Here by tooth and bloom and shell,*
> *Bubble, boil, blacken well!"*

Take the pot from its fire and allow it to cool. When it is as cold as a corpse, we'll bottle the brew into a small vial. Witches 'round here are rarely caught without a vial of the Black Brew on their person during the Twixtling days. They can be spotted most easily, for when they see a leaf break from its branch, the witches are the ones who will be darting towards it like a crack of lightning. If they can catch it before it touches the ground, they'll pull out their vial of Black Brew, pour this over the leaf, and speak their demands.

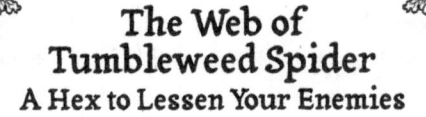

The Web of
Tumbleweed Spider
A Hex to Lessen Your Enemies

Nell Brimming was a witch, though no one spoke of it. This was a strict town with rigid permissions for anyone, especially the fringe folk. But Nell often worked to better us all, and without her doings in the night, many of us would have been much worse off. So, we kept our lips tight when it came to deals with the witch at the hickory corner of town.

But for me, I was on dire time that only one such as the witch could help me with. I went to the trees dressed in black, under the shadow of night when only the owls could see me. Though, when I knocked at her door, it seemed Nell already knew I was coming. She ushered me in, and I told her all about the troubles at my heels: how I'd become a target for Frances Coulbern, the wickedest woman in town. Her being the *richest* woman in town didn't help none either, since she never had to face any consequences.

The witch listened quietly to my woes with wide ears. As I spoke, she was quick at work. Nell dutifully tended the fire in her hearth and nestled a skillet onto the red coals. I asked her if she needed help, but she told me to keep talking. I continued, and as I spoke, I could feel myself begin to seethe with anger towards Frances.

As I told of the horrors that the wicked woman put me through, Nell filled the skillet with oil, and I watched her stir in several ingredients before it heated. Many of these were poisons that I recognized: jimson weed, pokeweed, and even the deadly water hemlock. I saw her stir in prickles, too, like greenbrier and thistle.

Lastly, she went to a large cobweb in the corner of her parlor. A spider sat in its center, and several other knots dotted the web—each a poor victim of the spider it seemed. Nell appeared to speak to the spider quietly as I ranted. And strangely so, the spider crawled off the web. Nell then collected the silk, knots and all, and threw this into the oil too.

I could hear the concoction begin to sizzle. At this point, the witch handed me a length of twine nearly as long as my arm. She said to tie as many knots in the twine as letters in Frances's name. And once this was done, I was to tie the twine into a loop. Then I would weave the twine between eight of my fingers, much like the cat's cradle game that kids would so often play on the pews. So, I did as was ordered, and as I wove, she chanted:

> *"Tumbleweed spider, thick as a knot,*
> *Coil my victim to wither and rot.*
> *Thistle and blister, dire and dread,*
> *Poison the wretch to lie as if dead.*
> *Tangle the webbing, loom and entomb,*
> *For only the spider to find and consume."*

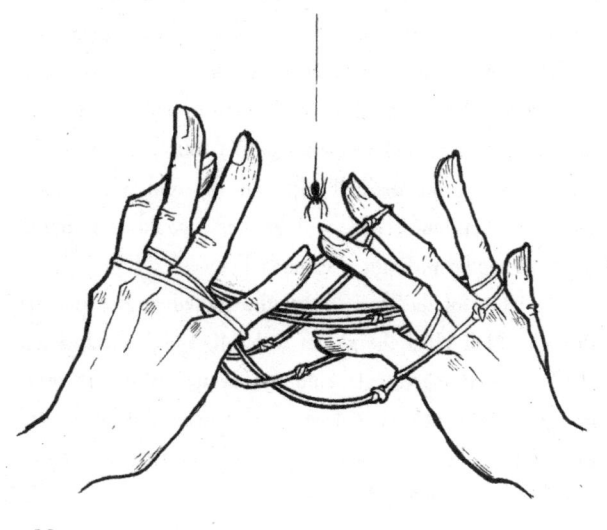

She repeated this a few times until the twine became a tangled knot. She told me then to gather all of my spite onto my tongue. I let it gather within my spit. When it began to burn, she told me to spit into the oil, and as it popped, to say the name of my victim. The knotted twine was to go into the oil next, and the charm was set.

She fished the knots out with a fireplace poker and folded them into a burlap swatch. Nell then gave me these next firm instructions: Under a dark sky when even the moon and stars could not be seen, I was to set fire to the knots until all that remained was ash. Then I must gather this ash and blow it into an occupied web so that the Tumbleweed Spider could consume my enemy.

I asked the witch who this Tumbleweed Spider was. She answered me first with a sly grin. Nell told me how prosy-folk, like me, have our churches and our angels, same as her. They only look different from time to time.

She was a mysterious one, that Nell Brimming. I'd see her now and again as always by the hickory corners of town. But Frances Coulbern, I'd not seen her the same way since. She seemed to lose her words in my presence, and even her skin grew pale as she neared. After a time, she didn't come by at all. For all I even knew, the Tumbleweed Spider had come to meet her for one last meal.

The Withy-With-Me
An Effigy to Feed Your Luck

Bo Voll was new to town. He had come from the north and brought with him a large family of bright-eyed children and a fair-haired wife. Their customs were strange, but that did not ostracize him. Here, everybody is from somewhere, and we all have our own customs to follow.

The days here can get hot as they are cold, which is to say *very*. Some days, a glass of water can be left on the porch for as long as it takes to trim a goat's hoof, and the air will drink it up before you have a chance. Even still, I'd often see Bo out by the lake on late afternoons plucking willow withies and rolling them into a satchel on his back.

I asked him once what he was doing. He answered me tentatively in a voice thicker than a bowl of hot oats, saying that he was feeding his luck. I thought, well heck, my luck could use a little feeding, too, and so I asked him to show me how it's done. Bo looked at me, unsure at first, but when he saw my interest was genuine, he nodded along and told me to pick a modest bundle of withies.

I followed him then, back to his little brick house by the train tracks. On the way, I found a small feather in the road. "This is a good sign," he said; my luck would favor me if I brought it with. When we got to his home, Bo ushered me into a shed behind the house. Somehow it seemed hotter in here than it was outside, but I was invested now.

Bo told me to strip the withies clean of leaves. He then told me to cut them down to a length somewhat near the height of my middle finger to my wrist. After that, I was to make two piles of the withies, then take the small feather I found and place it in the center of a bundle made from one of the piles. The second pile had to be bundled and tied with twine across the other like a cross.

I then had to split the bottom of the cross in two and use the twine to tie the halves in place. This item was now in the crude shape of a man. But the work was not yet done. Bo gave me three more lengths of twine: one in green, one in black, and one in red. He told me these represented the three provinces of my spirit and asked me to braid them together.

Once that was done, Bo took a clove of garlic from a bulb that hung by the shelves. He held this over the heart of the doll and instructed me to tie the braid over it so as to make an X that would hold the clove in place. Next to his workbench was a box of tools, from which he pulled a small iron carpet nail. As I held the doll, he began to press the nail through the braid and the clove, into the doll.

Lastly, Bo took a bottle of vinegar, ripe in scent, and wet his hands with it. He began to massage the liquid into the doll. As he did this, he spoke an incantation in his native tongue. I did not understand it at the time but have since altered his words to match my own. Here is what I say now—with some poetic license, I must admit:

"Hangman's twine take
bitter hold,
By iron knot of flaxen fold.
I set thee back, oh priest
of flies,
Steal no luck and tell
no lies.
Keep this fortune in
its place,
With sour wine to raise
its grace."

Bo told me that he learned to make this effigy from the old women who lived in his village back home. He said that it would hold my spirit of luck. If I can keep the effigy safe, my luck too will be safe. I must feed it a drop of vinegar mixed with my own essence once a month. If I can do this, my luck will gain strength.

I did as he said, and true enough, my luck quickly improved. I carry this doll everywhere I go and call it my "Withy-With-Me." I don't know much about this magic, nor the spirit that it feeds, but I do know that I am lucky to have met Bo Voll—and am getting luckier every day since.

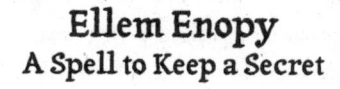

Ellem Enopy
A Spell to Keep a Secret

There is a legend here they people tell of a coyote with fur as sharp as spruce and claws sickled like the crescent moon. It loomed over houses as if it were the shadow of a thundercloud, waiting to burst with howls and lightning. The elders called it "Ellem Enopy," and its name was always said in dread for nothing could satiate its appetite. It ate flesh and bones as much as it did wood and iron. Whole buildings would have been devoured by the beast come morning.

But the elders had a plan for Ellem Enopy. They told the beast that they would feed it more than their towns could carry. It could eat anything that they spoke of. The great coyote was elated and took their offer. The first of our elders offered a field of cows and described it in such detail that the beast could smell the pastures. Ellem Enopy began to chew, and the cows promptly disappeared.

But the beast was not satisfied. And so, the second elder stepped forward, offering this time a grove of apple trees. Ellem Enopy again began to chew, and the woods disappeared, but it was not yet full. The third elder offered an entire mountain, and thus, the beast began to chew. Even still, the beast was not satisfied. Yet little did Ellem Enopy notice that it hadn't been eating substance, but stories. The elders were feeding it by reading from books whose pages were now empty—as was the beast's stomach, though it could not tell.

As the elders continued to feed the beast this way, it began to wither and shrink. After a time, all that was left of Ellem Enopy was a jawbone, eating stories, letters, and secrets from all who offered it such. But the beast must continue to be fed, lest it cease to eat letters and return to meals of substance. And so, even today we call upon Ellem Enopy to keep our secrets from prying eyes.

As our elders taught us, when the moon is thin, we are to take the jawbone of a carnivorous animal and write these letters upon it with black ink:

"LAP
MEO
NIN
OOM
PUL"

Then we are to tie a sprig of spruce around the bone with red thread and place it within a box. The box is to be seasoned well with a bed of spices such as salt, mint, ginger, and bee balm. Although some differ in their selection of spices, salt is always present. The box shall then be closed and a red candle burnt over top as we call the beast into the bone, saying:

"As blood is running red and warm,
Here the beast is given form.
By sprig of spruce and crescent sickle,
Yawning hunger, all but fickle.
Thin as a bone in
withered fetters,
Suck blood from these words and skin off these letters."

When the candle flickers, we know the beast is near. To hide a secret, we'll take a strip of untreated leather. Then using a brush and water, we write our secrets upon the skin. This must be placed into the box, sealed closed. Then we'll say:

"Ellem Enopy
Procks Gynth Blix Jewvd Zafqum
Eituzi! Eituzi! Eituzi!"

The skin shall be kept in the box, undisturbed, until the letters have faded from view. We know then that Ellem Enopy has eaten the words and our secrets will remain safe.

Afterword
Out of the Woods

Well, that wasn't so terrible. Beautiful Ophidia got just what she wanted, only at a price. The sly Ipscingen cleverly won his freedom, if in exchange for another's. Nonna Noxa got her due, and the brothers got theirs too. Aunty Black definitely made her mark on history, while Denna, Brynelda, and Pridge were all able to earn their titles as witches in their own ways.

The story's not over, of course. Witches are just the initiators after all. This is when things really begin. It's *your* turn now. The time has come for witchery. Although, when you face a need for magic most dire, remember the lessons of these witches. Or else the next Terrible might just be yours.

Terrible Storytelling

I t's said that fairy tales always have a grain of truth. Terribles, then, must have an entire boulder's worth. These tales, while at least partly fiction, are drawn from true stories in my own experience as a witch. Many of the spirits mentioned here are ones that do indeed exist, and these spells are based off real works of magic—although results may vary.

There is symbolism that goes into every story, just like how symbolism goes into every other work of art and, of course, every spell. The line that separates spells from stories can even be quite thin at times. Sometimes it's not there at all, if we don't want it to be. Maybe by reading this book, a new magic has been set loose, and you might begin to see things appear in your life because of it.

Having said all that, I want to share a little bit about the details hidden throughout *A Witches' Book of Terribles*. There is a lot of history in these pages that might be enjoyed by those who always try to find the hidden grains of truth. Or maybe just by those who have some spare time on their hands.

The Witch's Woods

The poem "Into the Witch's Woods" is what inspired this whole book. It is actually meant to be a story of mine and my brother Blake's adventures from when we found our magical similarities, to when we opened our witch's shop, and on to things we wanted to be able to do in the future. The poem itself is kind of about how we became witches. Or at least how our own witch paths came together. It's about our inspirations, our goals, important spirits we met, and magical milestones we passed. My hope is that this poem—and the rest of the book—can help guide other witches on their paths too.

Stripes and Spirals

Certain characters and their actions wear representative visual cues. Ones that hold true throughout the book are stripes and spirals. Witches in this book are always signified by wearing stripes in their outfit in one way or another. In a very abstract manner, these are supposed to represent roads or a witch's path. Nonna Noxa is the only one whose stripes are slightly obscured, because we do not know the true nature of her magic throughout the story.

On the other hand, acts of magic or the appearance of magical beings are signified with spirals. Those such as the Dismal Duenna or the Lackadaisical Hare have spirals worked into their outfit, atmosphere, and body. These shapes are often seen when witches are working their magic or when something magical is about to occur. Spirals are symbols of movement, working inward or outward depending on perspective. But on an even bigger scale than that, spirals mirror the shape of our galaxy. They are reminders that even the smallest snail shell can spin with the stars and tap into something bigger.

A Botanical Language

Flowers, leaves, nuts, and other herbs are used to frame many of the images in this book. As any green witch will tell you, plants have a language all their own. There is a reason why they are so common in spells. This is because the spirits in these plants—and the magic that they hold—can have the ability to tell your spell what it needs to do. As seen in these stories, plants are shown to give deeper insight into the characters' journeys and what may lie ahead for them. Drawing these herbs might even call their spirits into the ink as well. And just like that, a spell is cast!

Acorns: The most common plant shown in this book—as well as my own favorite magical ingredient—acorns are seen on this book's cover, the headers of every story, the introduction, and "Into the Witch's Woods." This is because the acorn is a symbol of beginnings. They represent childhood, wonder, potential, and initiation. It is also my belief that the gift of magic that witches have been given is represented in the acorn itself.

Birch and Clover: At the end of his story, Ipscingen is freed from the well and has cast a spell to find great fortune. Along with the mushrooms and buttercups (read their section below) signifying that he is back to business as usual, he is also walking on clovers to represent his good luck. Birch trees are behind him and framing the image, showing that he is free and the way before him is clear.

Bittersweet Nightshade: Aunty Black is symbolized by this beautiful vine. While poisonous, this plant is also alluring, which shows how she is seen by many in her borough. Like the plant, she is bitter and sweet, both a matter of interest and a possible threat. The nightshade is often found growing on fences and in hedges, which also represents Aunty Black as a hedge witch who is always between worlds.

Calla Lilies: This flower is used in many marriage ceremonies as a sign of devotion and union for the couple. Likewise, it is also used in funerals and to decorate tombs with symbols of rebirth. Here, the calla lily is a sign of Death who has come as the presider of the marriage ceremony but also bring an end to the brothers. Through the end of two lives and the beginning of one life shared, these virtues of rebirth are certainly present.

Chamomile and Belladonna: Dandy Duly's hood shows a stylized string of flowers. The small one is the chamomile, which is peaceful and overall harmless to people. The wider one is the belladonna or deadly nightshade, which can have disastrous effects. Both of the flowers strung up with a peach leaf represent Dandy's dual nature to "cast with both his hands."

Crocus: One of the first flowers to appear in the spring, crocus is seen in the swamp surrounding Nonna Noxa's house. This signifies a new beginning for Felix after his ordeal with the wicked witch.

Daffodil and Poppy: Pridge is framed by these two flowers in his story. While they often have positive attributes, they do not represent that here. The daffodil, a poisonous plant also known as "the Narcissus," symbolizes Pridge's self-absorption. The poppy is used in many extractions to promote sleep, and here, shows the boy's laziness.

English Ivy: Aunt Brynelda and her trowel are surrounded by a frame of English ivy. These vines are telling us that she has a strong bond with this tool. This is a symbol of everlasting loyalty and friendship between the two, as well as with the plants that Aunt Brynelda is using her magic on.

Hydrangea: When Ophidia confronts her family with her new self, it leads to her casting them away and abandoning her old life. This is symbolized by the hydrangeas, which represent vanity and boastfulness—traits that are taking over Ophidia's life. Hydrangeas are also used to represent someone who is bound to be alone. Its many colors likewise can represent the many faces that Ophidia wears. This flower is also known by the name "hortensia."

Mayapple: In the Introduction, "Enter the Crossroads," a path is seen with mayapple growing along its edge. This is known mostly as "American Mandrake," but its power goes beyond that. Its leaves are like several snakes' tongues, all trying to whisper a secret. Many mayapples are forked like a path with their fruit growing in the middle. And so here, the plant holds the power of choices along the crooked path that the witch is bound to follow.

Milkweed: The young witchling, Pridge, was given the task of making lace from milkweed in The Lackadaisical Hare. This plant is chosen, not only because it is so fibrous, but also because it is the food of the monarch caterpillar. For this magic, the milkweed works to aid Pridge is transforming from his larval state into a regal monarch. It is a plant of diligence and resilience, where through hard work, one can attain great heights.

Mushrooms and Buttercups: In Chapter Two, "Ipscingen of the Wishing Well," these represent Ipscingen's carefree nature. The wishing well is surrounded by fly agaric mushrooms and buttercups. The buttercup represents joy and youth, with Ipscingen jovially shrugging off his predicament. The fly agaric is a significant ingredient used in many cultures to bring about feelings of flight and the fairy folk, but also carries with it the dangers of death and entrapment.

Pilewort: Also known as the "lesser celandine," Hortense is seen walking over these flowers as the snakes slither around her. Pilewort is a flower that closes in darkness and opens in the light. This gives it a feature of invisibility, showing that Hortense feels invisible everywhere except when she is with the snakes. This flower has also been used in the past amongst beggars by rubbing the juice on their skin. This would produce sores, which in turn made them seem more pitiful to onlookers—a trait Hortense can relate to.

A Witch's Book of Terribles

Stinging Nettle: The princess has an equally dubious plant framing her. Stinging nettle, while not as lovely nor as poisonous as it is bittersweet, makes up for it with pain. Many may confuse the nettle with the proper mint at first glance, but if they touch it, they will quickly notice that it produces an agonizing sting and rash to match the princess's personality.

Thorns: When the gammer is defeated, she is framed by rose thorns, without the presence of any flower. Throughout this story, no flowers are drawn, meaning Aunt Brynelda is not a very showy person, unlike the gammer. When she finds the need to stand up for herself, however, she does put on a show, but she does this with the fierceness of thorns and not the beauty of a flower.

Wild Violets: Denna is surrounded by violets when she sings her spells. This is a symbol of childhood, harmony, and innocence to show the nature of her magic, as well as the excitement for magic that her sisters are experiencing. A darker side to violets, however, represents mourning over the death of the young, foreshadowing what is about to happen to her sisters.

Willow: When the gammer is said to grow taller and fuller over Aunt Brynelda, she envelopes her in her shadow. The grace and presence of this tree represents the gammer becoming more powerful. But the emotional nature of the weeping willow and the way its leaves droop represent the sorrow felt by the witch.

Witch Hazel: Appearing in the poem "The Bending Wood," witch hazel's flexibility is a symbol of secrecy and truth. Aunty Black is calling out to the truth that she needs to set things right, which shows that lies shall not be spoken, but that the truth is often bendable and may not come out as clearly as needed.

Wolfsbane: A plant long associated with transformation, especially relating to werewolves, wolfsbane surrounds Nonna Noxa when her true nature is finally revealed to Felix. Now that her white lace has been pulled back, he can see that she is a wolf in sheep's clothing.

Yew: An evergreen tree and shrub, yew is a symbol of wintertime. In his story, Felix is coming face to face with the troubles of this season on many levels. Yew, with its bright red berries and toxic nature is also a foreboding symbol of danger and death. This shows that Felix is venturing further into winter where he will come face to face with a deadly force. But, as yew also symbolizes, he goes through a state of rebirth by the end of it.

Appendix Two
A Magical Menagerie

For witches, everything has a spirit. Trees, hills, homes, and even time itself can hold the force of life. Whether we call them "spirits," "specters," "wights," or "faeries," we are in truth not much different than they are. The biggest wedge between us is that we are still held to mortal bodies. But that is only temporary. Witches themselves draw much of their power from blurring the lines of mortality. And many of the most powerful spirits are ones that were once witches themselves.

A lot of the beings in this book are such a spirit. I myself have come into contact with some of them. Others are inventions of the imagination. Although if that were to stop them from affecting the lives of myself and those around me, it hasn't happened yet. You may even have come into contact with some but called them by another name.

In these passages, I want to give space to these beings so that they can be more easily understood than quick words on the page.

Knotwood Sprites

These beings show up throughout these Terribles. They are ones that I often work with myself and who have appeared to me many times. I like to call them "Knotwood Sprites" because they most often reveal themselves to me as human features in the knots of trees. But they do sometimes show themselves in clouds, stones, grassy knolls, and beds of water.

I believe Knotwood Sprites are spirits of initiation and the ancestors of our magical lines. These might not be actual family members from our bloodlines but instead the manifestations of our magical sources coming to us. Whatever those sources are, when they appear in this world, our features mix with the natural world and take on a human likeness.

Aunt Brynelda is already a witch at the beginning of her story. Much of her magic is channeled through the relationship she has with the earth and her trowel. When the trowel is destroyed, she returns it to the earth, and a new source of her magic is born. She is then a force of nature herself, and the tree that grows over her becomes the Knotwood Sprite to mark this transformation.

Pridge and the other witches in Bosbury all visit the Oaken Wight to receive their familiar spirits and become initiated with their full potential. For these witches, the sprite doesn't appear just for them. It is a source of magic that preexisted, likely older than Bosbury itself. But when they found it, they recognized its power and continue to align themselves with it to access deeper currents of magic.

The Knotwood Sprites are also present at the Blood Wedding, along with several other magical beings. This congregation is a powerful event on its own, akin to what may be happening in the magical realms during an eclipse or a solstice. A Knotwood Sprite may very well be the doorway that allowed Casper and Pendleton to arrive at the wedding at all.

The Dismal Duenna

Described as a faerie, this creature is an immensely powerful phantasm well-learned in the ways of magic. Part of her story comes from a true experience I had with my brother. We were—and still are—pretty reckless with magic. Luckily, that is something that inspired a lot of stories in this book and will probably continue to inspire for many more reckless days.

In our experience, we were casting a whole string of spells in a house that the two of us rented for the weekend. One of the spells we cast was a potion to summon faeries, which spilled accidentally in the house. It might not be a surprise to learn that this went wrongly awry and caused a whole string of strange things to happen. Muddy footprints appeared in the middle of a room, items went missing, doors swung open, and appliances turned themselves on. While being fun to witness, it was quickly clear that we were in way over our heads. I'm not sure what we woke up in that house, or if it's still there, but that might have to be a story for someone else's Terribles.

The faerie in this story is not fun but does have the same lesson. She is here to show how summonings might not always turn out how we expect. Faeries especially get a very innocent reputation that should be unlearned as quickly as possible if you plan to work with them. The Dismal Duenna is not a being that I've met myself, but some of my other experiences with the fair folk have been closer to meetings with her than with a fairy godmother. Just remember that faeries and spirits, much like humans, come in all kinds.

The Hare

There are many kinds of spirits—some associated with animals—that we witches will often find a great deal of support from. One of these is the familiar, which Pridge encounters in Chapter Four, "The Lackadaisical Hare." These are spirits who are usually given to witches after an ordeal from more powerful beings. In folklore, these beings are often some form of the Devil, Faerie royalty, or coven leaders who grant the witch their familiar after their initiation. The familiar will then aid the witch, teaching them how to use magic and lending some of their own power to accomplish bewitching deeds.

I spent a long time looking for my own familiar and had many imaginings of what it would be. Not only did I not receive mine as a merit from another entity, but the spirit didn't actually rely on appearances either. He wore different shapes like they were dress codes at a dinner. Apparently, he chose his form for my convenience rather than his own, which didn't even end up being an animal at all. So, like Pridge soon understood, whether I was met by a hydra or a housefly, its appearance would not signify its nature.

The power he gave me wasn't what I expected either. At first, it was all just good advice. He would often talk to me in circles, giving answers before I knew what question to ask. It wasn't until the end of a conversation, when we ended up back at the beginning, that I even realized that something was learned.

Death and the Newly Bleds

Periwinkle Pennyknuckle and Waylon Blood have a few layers of meaning in their story. They are both spirits of place, who can be seen as rulers of the land in which they reside. Their wedding gathers all the other local spirits even as these two forces unite, culminating in a time of great magic.

This wedding is symbolic of what may happen among the spirits during powerful celestial events, seasonal turns, significant weather patterns, or pivotal anniversaries. The Blood Wedding may in fact be something that happens once every year from our point of view. It is an inevitable force of nature, which is why Death presides over it all.

The bride and groom are figures who I imagined while seeing random wildflowers popping up on the side of the road in early spring. They baked in my thoughts for a long time—along with the weedy Mallory Munchett—as small gods of the roadside wilds. It seemed like there was something so big in the ideas of the little worlds they carved out for themselves where the forces of nature were the least expected. At some point, it grew even bigger than my own mind when these figures became the names that the little wilds would take on when trying to get my attention.

Milk Mary May and Peppermint Tom

These quickly referenced attendants of the Blood Wedding are the names of sheep that I like to use in a method of divination when driving through the countryside. Milk Mary May is the name of white sheep, who represent the common fortunes of the day. Peppermint Tom is the name of black sheep, who represent an unexpected turn onto the crooked path. As with most things, I've prescribed this little fortune telling method in rhyme:

Should see the shepherd in his field, a count all so befitting,
To know the fortunes of his day from where and when he's sitting.
The shepherd looks onto his flock and gives his crook a pull,
On the end, Milk Mary May in white and golden wool.
Skies unchanged with eight or more,
Meet someone new with seven.
With six a journey by the shore,
With five a worry leavens.
With four take heed what you dreamed of,
And three, your pockets cleaned.
With two you'll find the one you love,
But one will bring a fiend.
Yet should you see within the flock, a speck of blackened fleece,
Know that only Devil's kin will find from this their peace.
For all the else, you best leave way, or mark a journey's end,
As Peppermint Tom has very few he deems to call his friend.

Nonna Noxa

Possibly once an average witch herself, Nonna Noxa seems to have rotted into something inhuman through the use of tainted magic and venomous pacts. She represents the toxic side of witchcraft and what may happen when a witch loses their values to their deeds. I fell into the dark sides of magic many times, casting wicked spells carelessly and treating vengeance like a midnight snack. I don't believe there is a good and evil to magic, but I do think it can take us too far to where we forget who we and become someone else.

I liked to imagine this in Nonna Noxa as being a swamp witch during the early nineteenth century American Midwest. She is the combination of three venomous animals: spiders, frogs, and snakes. The witch brews enchanted poisons made by corrupting the innocence of children and harvesting their foulness into a witch's venom she uses to cast her spells.

Even though the witch is ultimately defeated, I don't imagine her as ever being gone. Corruption will always exist. It might shed its skin and become something new every once in a while, but Nonna Noxa will still roam the land, looking for more innocence to harvest her poisons from.

The Gray Crone

The entity in "The Pramby Stone" that taught Gammy the method to use her signature form of magic is actually much more powerful than she is given credit for in this story. The Gray Crone is my interpretation of a real spirit that I have met many times around the Midwest. She is the spirit of Lake Michigan as I have seen her.

I believe that the waters of a land move as its lifeblood, and the tide waters that ebb and flow are its heart. Lake Michigan itself is the source of life for the spirits that gather around it. But she is also as fierce as she is nurturing.

In the aforementioned story, the lake is depicted as ominous and haggard. This is because she represents the lake spirit during the colder months, when the waters become gray and violent. This version of the lake I like to call "Mary Grim"; she is ravaged with hunger and will undoubtedly drag in and kill anyone who gets too close during this time. But during the warmer months, she is peaceful and welcoming in bright shades of blue. I like to call this side of her "Fair Mera."

Still, both versions of the entity seem to be in a constant state of hunger. If you float in the warm waters long enough, she'll lure you out where it's too far to swim back. But while she still has sinister intent and wouldn't think twice about eating you, Fair Mera seems more well-fed than her counterpart—and thus will grant good fortune to those who approach. Mary Grim on the other hand is much more desperate and deals out despair to show for it. So, like Gammy, I will often visit Mary Grim in the winter and offer her a cut of bloody meat to keep her satisfied. This seems like enough to stave off her misfortune for a few months at least.

Tumbleweed Spider

In my experience, I've found that spiders are more than happy to make deals with witches. If given a warm place to build their webs and catch their food, there is a surprising amount of magic they can help us with. Most commonly, I employ spiders as guardians of my home. Sometimes, it feels like they are the house spirits themselves—or at least its emissaries—sending me messages and testing our deal.

The spell of Tumbleweed Spider, however, delves into some of the spider's more depraved aspects. In some of the rituals we've worked at our shop-held gatherings, we practiced the spell of Tumbleweed Spider. This ritual was labeled as an "unsavory kind" and not meant for casual casters, of course. Those who attended were told to only come if they had an enemy to undo and spite to spend, as long as their ethics had room for what might come.

While not the most wretched of curses, Tumbleweed Spider is an awfully effective hex and can cause plenty of damage in the right hands. Like I said, I believe the spiders represent spirits of the home. But just because I believe it doesn't make it true. And sometimes I do worry about who I am sending my enemies towards and what actually happens to them once they fall victim to Tumbleweed Spider's web.

The End